BETTY LOCKYER was born on 17 March 1942 at Beagle Bay Mission in the Kimberley Region of Western Australia. Descended from the Nyul Nyul people of the Dampier Peninsula, Betty was a 'war baby' and spent her early years at the mission as one of the evacuees from Broome. When she was four years old, she returned to Broome and lived at the Holy Child Orphanage before being reunited with her mother and family.

In 1956 she became the first Aboriginal student from the Kimberley to attend St Brigid's College in Perth. She left Broome for good in 1958 to work in Port Hedland at the Postmaster General's Office.

Betty lived in Port Hedland for many years and worked in the area of Indigenous Health as a community worker. In 2003 she moved to Perth to study Health Promotion. She is the mother of eleven children, has thirty-nine grandchildren and sixteen great-grandchildren.

LAST TRUCK OUT

BETTY LOCKYER

Magabala Books

First published in 2009, reprinted 2010, 2015, 2018, 2019, 2020
Magabala Books Aboriginal Corporation, Broome, Western Australia
Website: www.magabala.com Email: sales@magabala.com

Magabala Books receives financial assistance from the Commonwealth Government through the
Australia Council, its arts advisory body. The State of Western Australia has made investment
in this project through the Department of Local Government, Sport and Cultural Industries.
Magabala Books would like to acknowledge the generous support of the Shire of Broome,
Western Australia.

The views expressed in this publication are those of the author and not necessarily those
of Magabala Books Aboriginal Corporation. The publisher has made every effort to contact
copyright owners for permission to use material reproduced in this book. If material has been
used inadvertently without permission, please contact the publisher.

Designed by Jo Hunt
Printed and bound in Australia by Ovato Print Pty Ltd
National Library of Australia
Cataloguing-in-Publication data
Lockyer, Betty (Elizabeth), 1942-
Last truck out / Betty Lockyer.

ISBN 9781921248085 (pbk)
Lockyer, Betty (Elizabeth), 1942 – Childhood and youth.
Orphans – Western Australia – Beagle Bay –Biography.
Parental deprivation – Western Australia –Broome.
World War, 1939-1945 – Evacuation of civilians – Western Australia – Broome.
Beagle Bay Mission (W.A.) – Social life and customs.

305.23086945092

For my grandparents, Alice and William Wright, who found freedom amidst their spiritual sorrow.

❖

ACKNOWLEDGEMENTS

Thank you to the people and family who have helped me along this journey to tell my story. Special thanks to Sue Kenworthy who sat with me way back in the mid-1990s and encouraged me to start writing. Thanks also to Odette Hayley, Cathy Donnelly, Trudy Hayes and Nancy Brown who gave up their time to read early drafts and provide feedback.

Thanks to my daughter, Sylvia, who spent many hours talking with me about my story and gently reminded me about important family anecdotes that should be included. And special thanks to Margy, my sister, who worked very hard to find family photographs.

Thanks also to Bruce Sims and Magabala Books who were a pleasure to work with to bring my story to publication.

This book contains names and photographs of people
who have passed away, which may cause sadness
to some people.

The Dampier Peninsula and the Broome region
is home to Aboriginal people from different
language groups. In the 1880s the establishment
of the pearling industry brought workers to
Broome from many Asian countries, creating a
cosmopolitan town unlike any other in Australia.

Words from other languages, both Aboriginal
and Asian, have therefore found their way into the
local vernacular, and sometimes their origins are not
clear. In *Last Truck Out*, words other than English
are in italics when first mentioned. Their common
interpretations are to be found in the Glossary.

CONTENTS

INTRODUCTION

This is about a once young Aboriginal woman's belongingness to Beagle Bay and Broome, Kimberley Country, Western Australia.

Depending on the era, the words native, full blood, Indigenous and Aboriginal are used at different times for different reasons. They were widely and loosely used in the past but Indigenous people today may find them to be offensive. Although the word Indigenous covers both Aboriginal and Torres Strait Islanders (TSI), we are distinct races. I prefer to use Aboriginal for my people and, with respect, I cannot speak for TSI people as I do not know their story.

A lot of the people mentioned have passed on into another life but sometimes people need to be known and acknowledged in the Western way for our own stories and history. Sometimes one has to take a walk back into the past to see what was being done then and come back into the present to see if much has been achieved.

My grandparents, William Wright and Alice Kotonel, were raised on the Catholic-run Beagle Bay Mission as displaced native children from the late 1890s and early 1900s. They married in the Sacred Heart Mission Church on the 31st of May 1919.

From this marriage they produced eight daughters: my mother Agnes, and her sisters, Elizabeth, Kathleen, Margaret, Christina, Isobella, Philomena and Cecilia. All were born in Beagle Bay.

According to the Department of Native Welfare records, William was born to George Wright, white man, and an unknown native woman and taken to the mission from the East Kimberley.

Alice was born to an unknown father, possibly Asian, and Maudie, a full blood woman from the Beagle Bay area.

We were known by our father's name; thus I was Betty Hussan for a long time. When I grew older I was told to use my registered name of Wright. Most of the kids still used their fathers' names even up to the time they got married.

I use the Broome-talk language I grew up with, how people talked in those days. It's not making fun of the way we speak. I still revert to the talk whenever I go back to Broome or meet up with Broome people. It is uniquely Broome.

I wrote this book for my siblings, children and grandchildren because I have never told them much about my childhood; they could only imagine it. When I tried to tell some of my children years ago, one of them asked, 'Were you a girl, Mum? It can't be; you're our mother.' I felt no good. I should have told them from baby time.

As we always say, 'You have to know where you come from, know where your people come from, even if they were forced to leave their homelands and you, many years ago. You have to know country. Otherwise you will never be at peace, never experience the belongingness of family.'

Whenever I travel back to Broome by car, I have this eerie feeling of apprehension and anticipation creeping into me. This must be the feeling of coming home.

The red pindan landscape, the wooded bush, the bulldust of the Roebuck Plains, the smell of the ti-trees, the cattle roaming or resting under their shade, all bring memories and images of old Broome town.

As I get nearer the town, I can smell the saltwater and wet marsh. From there come images flashing through my mind of the old ramshackle houses huddled snugly together, the flooded marsh with the little heads of the down-the-marsh kids bobbing along.

Sometimes I take a ride around Chinatown to see if the place has changed, hoping to see the Sun Pictures, Streeter jetty and other landmarks as they were, but time waits for no one. Sadly, there are no 'down-the-marsh' kids any more and only some old familiar friends and family walking around.

Regardless of now living elsewhere, I still feel at home.

'Grange', Betty Lockyer

BEAGLE BAY
MISSION

LAST TRUCK
OUT

LAST TRUCK OUT! This is the last truck for us to clear out and head for Beagle Bay.' Those were the commanding words of Uncle Benda Mathews. 'If we don't go now, the bombs might surely kill us!'

News went around Broome that attacks might occur any day because the enemy was snaking its way down the Asian countries and getting closer to Australia. By the 17th of February 1942, everyone was ready and the truck was the last chance to get out. That made up their minds quick smart, thus the hurried preparation for the trip, and indeed Darwin was bombed only two days later on the 19th of February.

With the air raid and bombing of Darwin there was grave and immediate concern for the possible invasion of our northern ports, particularly the Western Australian coastline, the most vulnerable point of invasion to this country. No one wanted to be caught napping like the Americans had in Hawaii with Pearl Harbour. The military authorities decided to remove the coloured population from the northern ports for evacuation to isolated areas such as the Beagle Bay Mission, run by the German order of the Pallottine Brothers and the St John of God Sisters, located 120 kilometres north of Broome. Most of the native people thought they'd be safer in Beagle Bay anyway.

When World War II had first broken out in Europe in 1939, it had been anticipated that the German missionaries might be interned. The Pallottine Brothers had been in Beagle Bay since the turn of the century. Who was going to say Mass and hear confessions, they asked each other? To where could those missionaries escape anyway? They were dedicated and committed to the missionary life and their Aboriginal people, not to warfare. Most of them wanted to be buried on the mission when they died and only a few wanted to go back to Germany on their retirement. Such was their affinity with the Aboriginal people, their land and the spirituality they had experienced in their lives. Their hearts were in the Kimberley.

Even though our mob knew that they had to leave Broome, they were still waiting till the last minute to get ready. Uncle Benda was rushing the women and children to hurry up. Time was running out and he wanted to get them to a safer place. Everyone had been advised only to take the necessary goods. Mum and Aunty Barb had made up their minds to take their trusty old Singer treadle machines, because they didn't know how long they'd be gone. They treasured their sewing needles, reels of cotton, scissors and materials. Things were hard to come by in those times and they had to be prepared for the future. Every scrap of anything was saved. Goodness knows how long the war would last.

Uncle had already driven others out to the mission. Back and forth he drove, perhaps driven by panic or just gravely concerned

BEAGLE BAY TRUCK, CHINATOWN, BROOME, 1940s

for the safety of his family and countrymen. All these women and men were classed as 'evacuees' even though Beagle Bay Mission was considered their home, having been raised there as children.

This group of people was one of the last to leave. Little did they know that Broome would be bombed just days later and that further attacks were anticipated.

Broome had become a stopover port for the Dutch people leaving Java and other parts of Indonesia to escape the Japanese invasion. On the morning of March the 3rd their flying boats, or seaplanes, were blown out of the water in Roebuck Bay and many men, women and children lost their lives. They were buried in the Dutch cemetery overlooking the big jetty and Roebuck Bay.

On this last truck was Uncle Benda, his wife Aunty Willa and their sons: Mickey and Terry. There was also Garda Howard and her son Alex who was about three months old and Aunty Barbara Drummond and her two-year-old daughter Pearl. Aunty Barb was also *bugunjun* with twins Sally and Jimmy. Then there was my mum Agnes Wright who wasn't a mum yet, because she was still carrying me. I believe that there could have been Granny Teresa Torres and her young children in the group as well.

My *mimi* Alice Wright was also there as she had been living in Broome for a couple of years. She was one of the many unofficial midwives for both the women of Beagle Bay and Broome. Women in Broome would send a message to her via the bush telegraph and sometimes she could be booked out for months. Women placed their trust in her for they knew that there would be no reporting procedures or follow-ups. She may not have been a trained midwife but she had the skills and experience of a traditional bush woman in delivering babies. The women believed and relied on bush medicine and remedies. To them, Indigenous medicine was more about treating through spiritual healing and physical healing by bush medicine, plants and foods and fruit. They wanted all those things to ease the pain. When it came to birthing, they wanted their own mob.

Mimi was in great demand for her birthing skills. She had delivered Aunty Barb's first baby on New Year's Day 1940 and she was asked to name the child. She showed Aunty Barb a pearl that Mrs Male in Broome had given her for Christmas and so the child was named Pearl. Mimi felt it was a good omen, even though the pearl she had been given must have been a baroque (irregular shaped pearl). How ironic, for many years later, Pearl and her husband became the owners of a flourishing cultured pearl business in Broome.

Mum and Aunty Barb were glad that Mimi was travelling with them in case they might have an early delivery. One can only imagine how those two bugunjun women managed to get onto the truck that was packed. There were no ladders or forklifts.

ON THE ROAD TO BEAGLE BAY, 1950s

'Yeah, poor fella, poor fella,' Aunty Barb told Sally and me lots of times over the ensuing years. 'Your mummy and I were bugunjun. Aggie was nine months with little Betty and I was eight months with Sally and Jimmy. Nobody told me I was having two babies at the same time. Twins, mind you. God knows it, I didn't know anything! Yeah, Japanese planes were bombing Broome in March. I remember that because little Betty was born on St Patrick's Day and I had my two in April. We made it to Beagle Bay just in time, thank God. We also had to buy one nanny goat for milk for the little ones. Yeah, that nanny goat was treated like a queen, sitting right on top of the truck with us, never mind *goomboo* smell all the way, with wind blowing in our faces. We had to mind it like it was our own baby, like it was gold. Lucky we knew how to milk that nanny goat from our convent days.'

My mum took up the story, reliving those days on the road.

'It took us days to get to the mission, but it seemed like months. I don't know how many breakdowns we had, punctures nearly every mile, radiator boiling, everything going wrong. We'd camp for days at a time, and then move on. Talk about mosquitoes and sand flies! All the little ones had to sleep under mosquito nets hanging from a tree branch, with us sitting outside near the campfires, trying to smoke out the mosquitoes. We had a few kerosene lamps around us too, burning all night. You know what kind we get, frightened for any kind things. We just had to leave the lamps burning. Poor *bublee* Benda, he had to mind all his *jidjas*.'

'There were lots of other travellers on the road all heading for one place, us passing them, them passing us, taking turns and turns. Your Uncle Jacob Sesar was travelling in another truck, so we were right. We had other company most of the time,' said Aunty Barb.

Uncle Jacob was to marry my Aunty Kudjie just before the war ended. She was Kathleen, Mum's third eldest sister.

It must have been a frightening time for our mums, especially mine, because I was her first-to-be-born child. The other women already had their first-born children, but not my mum. She was only in beginner's class. I was also the first grandchild in the family. True, I wasn't aware of all this excitement going around me and because of this I have gathered many stories and entries from my family's files to help me build mind pictures about how things must have been in the wartime era in Beagle Bay and Broome.

In all my reading and research, I have found hardly any mention or recognition given to the native people's influence and occupations in wartime Broome, or even to their loyalty as housemaids and handymen to their employers. The same applies to the Asian people who had made Broome their home.

Since the 1880s the thriving pearling industry had attracted indentured seamen from many Asian countries, such as Malaya, China, Indonesia, and Japan. Broome's pearling industry was built upon the labour, loyalty, integrity and seamanship of these Asian and Aboriginal workers.

Before the war, people in Broome were ordinary people going about their daily lives. Everyone knew each other; everyone shopped at the same shops and dealt with other small businesses in town in the same way. They bought and sold goods. They laughed and cried together. There may have been different levels of Broome society but life went on regardless in this sleepy little seaside haven. Natives and Asians made friends and got along and that was the way it was. Then along came this horrible war and all of a sudden Broome was a town divided, where bitterness and hidden feelings came out in the open and where those feelings sure ran high. Such people showed themselves for what they really were in terms of racism and their loyalty to Britain.

Many of the Japanese men had married native women and they, with their little children, were interned and taken over east and elsewhere. There was a war with Japan and Germany and internment for those nationals was inevitable, but many Aboriginal people wondered why their wives and children were taken away as well. They were removed from their own country and placed in a strange environment, thousands of miles away.

The majority of shops and stores in Broome were closed down, boarded up and left as they were. The owners of the two Japanese department stores, Tonan & Shokai Department Store and the Gengi Department Store, together with the Japanese pearlers had been interned. Looting was rampant and no shop was left intact with its merchandise. Wartime feelings ran high, so eventually the two stores were razed to the ground but not before the 'goodies' were taken.

'Poor fella Mrs Gengi. Poor fella my friend,' Aunty Barb told us sorrowfully. 'They took her away. No more Mrs Gengi. She was a harmless old thing.'

A few days before the group left for Beagle Bay, Georgy Howard went to Aunty Barb's place and gave Pearly a big teddy bear and a toy tea set.

'Where you got those things from, boy? Don't tell me you been robbing the shops, too?' asked Aunty.

'Don't worry, *jidja* Barb! Everybody's robbing in town. You should see them *gardias* and *linjus*. They're all taking stuff. Them linjus can't say anything to us. They're helping themselves, too. You go and see for yourself,' replied Georgy.

I often wonder how many other treasures found their way into homes around the country and how many of those treasures are still around today.

A few Japanese families did return to Broome after the war but others never made it back. Some of their children and grandchildren eventually found their way home to see their grandmother's country many, many years later. Our people had always wondered about what had happened to those families and friends who were taken away. With their descendants returning to their country, the Broome people found some closure at last.

Our mums told us many stories about the 'funny' things that happened through those despairing times. Not all stories were doom and gloom.

Although arrangements were made for the Broome population to evacuate the town, there were some who elected to stay. They had to 'go bush' during the day and return in the safety of the night. Most evacuees who went to the mission returned to Broome when it was safe but others stayed for a longer period.

One such person who tagged along with the evacuees, was an old Chinaman. He was Ah Ming but everybody called him Anawai. He was well known and liked by the natives because he was one of the few shopkeepers who let them book up goods when they were broke. They paid up when they had money again, from either working or gambling.

'More better you go Beagle Bay, not Derby. *Bumbye* you die when bomb drop. Everyone knows you there. More better you follow us to mission,' Uncle Benda and Uncle Jacob told him.

After much persuasion and because he trusted those people,

he went and bought himself a donkey and cart and loaded it up with tinned meat, tinned fruit, tinned butter, flour, rice, fresh fruit and vegetables, eggs and whatever else he could carry. He had to lock up his store and hope it was still there when they'd be allowed back in town. Then off he went, following the travellers, not knowing much about the donkey business or bush country.

Anawai would pull up near the others and camp a short distance away. During the night some of his food was stolen by some person or persons unknown. Morning came and everyone could hear one old Chinaman going off his head, shouting hysterically, in a mixture of Chinese and broken-down English.

'Ahya! Ahya! Someone pinchee my food! Someone pinchee my flootee! Eblee night happen. I catchee, I hittee! No good *binghi*! No good binghi!' Then he'd go running to Uncle Benda and Uncle Jacob.

'Mr Benda! Mr Jacob! Binghi stealee my food. Eblee night stealee something. Today stealee eggs. Yes'day stealee tin meat. Tomollow stealee flootee. No good binghi! No good binghi!'

The pinching went on and old Anawai still couldn't catch the binghi robbers. So when the storytelling went around the campfires of an evening, you can easily guess who headed the list. Even though they sympathised with him, they could see the funny side of it all. There were always actors amongst the storytellers and they sure acted out the scene to the hilt, with the sounds of the rolling laughter going on and on right into the night. By the time everybody reached the mission, old Anawai had only half a load left. Poor old Anawai!

Another story our mums told us about was when they were closer to the mission, near Bowen's Well. The truck broke down again. It was marshy country and they were stuck in the middle of nowhere, desperately trying to repair a puncture.

'Shoo! Shoo! You guys can't hear 'em? Sound like aeroplane engines coming,' yelled my mum.

Sure enough, there was the drone of aircraft, presumably the enemy, coming closer and closer. So they all jumped up with fright, scurrying around like rats, picking up things and throwing them onto the truck.

Kids were screaming and mums were yelling, 'Yor yor! Hurry up! Hurry up! We gonna get bombed!'

Imagine the sight! An old truck with a punctured tyre, Uncle Benda trying to drive it, women and children yelling with fright, all trying to help by pushing it under the cover of trees, two bugunjun women trying to push it as well, Anawai with his donkey, flogging it to make it move but no go! All the women were yelling at him to hurry it up. Goodness, it sure must have been a stubborn donkey or mule breed.

In all that confusion, they still managed to look up to the blue sky and saw planes flying very, very high and almost directly above them. Maybe the enemy planes did spot them, maybe not. Perhaps they were our own planes. No one looked up to identify the markings on the planes. Nevertheless, all they knew was that they were warplanes and that was good enough for them to take cover. They pondered about that for years, never really knowing the answer and not really wanting to know it, either.

'Well, we don't know how we got everything under cover, but we did it. Even old Anawai's donkey and cart got hidden in time. We must have got strength from fright. That must have been how we moved the truck, too,' said Uncle Benda.

'God was with us that day. We were all praying for dear life. He was with us for sure. He made sure we were well hidden,' piped in Aunty Willa.

It wasn't long before the truck was ready to roll again.

12

God sure must have been with them all right, because they had no more trouble after that. Only old Anawai had trouble trying to manage his donkey. In his haste to get to the mission and probably worrying about his goods, he flogged the poor old thing until it dropped dead in its tracks, just a few miles from the old mission. He was helped to get to the mission by the men.

No one was ever caught out for the overnight thieving but a lot of guessing went on amongst the people and some of them probably knew who were responsible for it, anyway.

As for my mum, mimi, aunties and Uncle Benda, once they smelt the ti-trees and heard the sounds of the *leret* they knew they were home free. They had made it to the safety of the mission. If they were to be bombed, at least they'd die in their own country.

When they arrived, they were either allocated housing or made their camps a little further away near Bernard's Well and Bishop's Well. The missionaries did not turn them away when they sought refuge but they had to live by the rules and hopefully in harmony with the mission community. It was a tight squeeze, but they shared whatever they had with each other, going fishing

BROOME WAR EVACUEES AT BEAGLE BAY MISSION, 1940s

and hunting to replenish their meagre supplies. According to records kept by the mission authorities, the number of evacuees fluctuated between 61 and 69, children included.

Once again Mum was reunited with her family and her sisters. There she waited until I was born. By right she was not meant to be in Beagle Bay and it was only because of the war that she was allowed to stay. She and my dad, Eusop bin Hussein (also spelt Yusep bin Hussan) had been in a relationship since 1939.

Before the war, about 1937, when she and Aunty Betty had both left the mission, they went to Derby to work for a time. While there they had to be examined by the doctor because Derby was a leprosy endemic area and one member of the family had already contracted the disease. They went on to Port Hedland to work and that was where Aunty met and married Uncle Gerry Clarke. Mum came back to Broome but Aunty stayed and brought up her children in Port Hedland. It was around about this time that Mum and Dad got together.

Dad was a diver from Malacca (he was not a Koepanger as stated in official files) who worked for Streeter & Male. Mum and Dad were brought before the court numerous times for cohabiting. It was an offence for native women to consort or cohabit with white men or men other than native. This was in a section of the 1905 Aborigines Protection Act.

The native women bore the brunt of their 'illicit' relationships with Asians and white men. It was a 'secret life' that many were forced to live but although they thought it was secret it was not so. Their every movement was recorded from information given to the authorities by informants who reported on their lives.

Mum and Dad did not deny their relationship and because of this they were hounded with raids on my mimi's house. There were also night raids on other native women in their homes.

On 24th December 1941, a court hearing was held and an extradition order for Mum to be removed from Broome to Moola Bulla Station was in place. The Department of Native Affairs wanted her case to be an example to other native women who cohabited with Asians or white men. They tried to get my father deported back to Malacca but the order was rejected and deferred until after the war as Australia was gearing up for the Pacific–Asia conflict. Thankfully, the deportation order never materialised.

While waiting to be taken to Moola Bulla, my mother's situation changed. Because of the war, she was to be allowed to stay at the mission as it was deemed too expensive an exercise in transportation.

Mum was also pregnant with me and I can only imagine what she and Dad were going through. They were to be first-time parents ever for their only child Elizabeth.

MY MOTHER, AGNES WRIGHT

A transcript written on April of 1942 reads:

At Beagle Bay Mission on Sunday last, I met two other Asiatic men, Eusop bin Hussein, attached to Agnes Wright and (...blank...) attached to (...blank...). They had been taken out to Beagle Bay by Barney Dean in a small motor vehicle belonging to Chapple's. One contended that Commander Davis of the Navy had given him permission to visit the mission. The other said he had understood I had given him permission.

However, I ordered them back to Broome and will call them in when they arrive. Incidentally, Agnes Wright gave birth to her child about three weeks ago. The Sergeant of Police informs me that there is a suggestion of sending her to Moola Bulla. In view of the fact that I will now be in a position to stop these visits of Asiatics to the Mission, I do not think the expense of transporting this girl to the Station would be necessary.
M Knight, Native Affairs 1st April 1942–extract.

The blanks or white-outs in the letters are to protect the identity of other people not related to our family.

In a reply to that letter the Commissioner of Native Affairs agreed with Mr Knight's recommendation under the present circumstances that no attempt be made to effect Agnes Wright's removal to Moola Bulla Government Station...signed and dated 1st April 1942.

The reason the Navy gave permission to the Asiatics and others was that the Military took command in the war situation and the Navy was in charge of the pearling fleet. My dad had wanted to see his child and still entered the mission on occasions by some means or other.

I suppose Native Affairs did have a hollow victory after all. I found out from the files that after about five years of separation from Mum, despite rendezvous during that time my father married a white woman in a 'marriage of convenience' but soon afterwards the marriage was dissolved. Despite this marriage, my parents kept their relationship until Dad went to Darwin to work. All up they were together for nearly ten years. By the same token, I don't believe that Mum would have married a divorced man anyway.

These same strict rules also applied to legal marriages with people other than natives, although it did seem that approval from the church for marriages between native women and Filipino men were more likely to be granted. The Filipinos were Catholics, assuring that the children would be brought up in the faith. There were other mixed marriages approved by the state and church but it was a slow process.

The alternative was for natives to apply for the Certificate of Exemption or a citizenship certificate so they could marry. Some people said that they'd never apply for it because they'd never deny their identity; others used it to their advantage but still retained ties with their native relations. If we get them papers, we can get things more easily for our mob, they said. The authorities didn't have to know. They stick together, we stick together.

My mother applied, but was refused on the grounds that:

> The Hon. Minister for the North West is unable to approve of the issue of a Certificate of Exemption to you. This decision is due to the necessity for precautionary medical reasons owing to your father's illness and because it is generally inadvisable for welfare reasons, to issue a Certificate of Exemption to you or that you should leave the environment of the North Commissioner of Native Affairs 2nd August 1942–extract.

In a letter to Const T.E. Jensen, Protector of Natives in Derby, the Commissioner of Native Affairs advised him of Mum's application having been rejected.

The Commissioner of Native Affairs stated that apart from the health issue:

> *The issue of a certificate seems inadvisable for general welfare reasons as well. Agnes was recently at the mission. She thus associated with natives to a recent date and since she also associated at one time with an Asiatic and has a child by him, it would appear to be generally inadvisable to issue a Certificate to her.*
> Commissioner of Native Affairs 2nd August 1942–extract.

Mum was evacuated to Beagle Bay Mission in 1942 and left to work in Derby in 1945, so of course she associated with natives on the mission. It was a native mission and she could not have possibly avoided fellow natives and their families. She was also still paying the price for her association with the 'Asiatic'. The Native Affairs and Holy Child Orphanage, in written communications, had said that the only reason Mum wanted the exemption certificate was so that she could marry Eusop because he was getting better wages and could support them.

Generally, the unattached native women were labelled as native prostitutes whether or not they were living with Asian men or white men. Prostitution may have been rife in the town but not all native women were such. In general terms, prostitution is payment in return for sexual favors. It would seem that people in Broome had this mindset that native women were exploited by the Asians. Sure, some women may have been taken advantage of by some Asians but keep in mind that there were half-white and quarter-white children running around in this country (over east) long before the half-Asian children joined them.

People tend to think that Aboriginal women were used only to harbour the Asian's sexual frustrations. They forget that those women took those men for their husbands or partners (common law) because they had fallen in love. They had created a loving family environment, bringing children into the world but were constantly harassed by the authorities, as were Mum and Dad.

One woman even asked the Native Affairs, 'How is it that we cannot live together when he minds us, gives us tucker, housing and clothes for the children like other people?' This was found in Mum's file but the other woman's name was blanked out.

It is a sensitive subject but many children from that era have read files on their parents (especially their mother's) and are deeply hurt by what was documented by Native Affairs.

At school some of us were referred to as 'illegitimate children of Asiatics'. I didn't know what the word meant but it made me feel uncomfortable, like it was a dirty word. I think I must have been about eight when I first heard it and it made me go cold. I knew what it meant when I finally could use a dictionary.

A large number of such documents were compiled by obtaining information from loose-mouthed townspeople and other informants. There were genuine loving relationships between couples and they were forced to live together outside of a marriage union. In most cases the proposed marriages of such people were not allowed by the church because the majority of Asians were Muslims or else the Native Affairs did not see fit for such marriages to occur. The general opinion was that native women should marry their own native men, but from where did those half-caste and quarter-caste people come in the first place? There were three strikes against those women, political, religious and just being native women.

These couples were forced to live in fear of authority. The men were fined but it was the women who paid the price of love. They were usually sentenced, then sent away to faraway places, such as Moola Bulla Station, the missions or down south. Their children were taken away as well and they could be sent to places other than where their mothers were sent, sometimes never being re-united. A classic case was my mum's.

Those women also lived with dreadful fear of their babies being taken from them straight after birth. They gave birth either in the bush or at home for fear of Native Affairs taking their babies away and never seeing them again. Most of their babies were never registered at the courthouse either, which proved to be a big headache when they went looking for birth certificates to get married or obtain passports to prove their existence.

I know of one bloke who wanted to get married and met with this problem in the 1950s. The Clerk of Court told him, 'As far as I'm concerned, you're not even born yet, so come back when you are.' Anyway that was sorted out through church records and he did get married in church.

If the women gave birth in the hospital they were duly reported to the Native Affairs if the babies were of different colour or looks other than Aboriginal. In the case of some legally wedded couples, if the husband was absent at the birth, it was presumed that the child was not his because the child was born during the time he was away working!

There was an incident relating to the hospital that happened when I was a child. I was admitted to the Broome District Hospital (BDH) and had an operation on my upper leg for a huge *bundagurr*. Anyway, the next day I was taken to the Native Hospital because natives could not be admitted to BDH as patients, unless it was a matter of life and death. As soon as the Matron saw me she ordered me back to the BDH. Again I was sent back to the Native Hospital. Some staff said I was native and the others said I was a half-caste Malay. An argument broke out between the hospitals deciding what caste I was. I was totally confused. It was finally decided that I could stay at the BDH.

I didn't care if I was half black, half white, half Malay or a half spotted cat. I just wanted my leg to heal.

In 1945, Mum went to Derby again for employment with Mr Gilbert King, the headmaster at the government school. The Kings had two young sons and Mum looked after them as well as being the domestic hand. This situation did not go down well with the Native Affairs because she did not apply through them. It was arranged by the mission authorities, I believe, and apparently there was a breakdown in communication. Seeing that she was already working in Derby the Native Affairs allowed her to stay.

When the Kings went to Perth on their school vacation, they wanted Mum to accompany them as their child carer but were refused. Mrs Edna King who had supported her husband in this matter, received this letter:

> *Dear Madam...I regret it is not possible to give you permission to bring Agnes Wright to Perth, or for that matter to any place South of the 20th parallel. Under Section 9A of the Native Administration Act 1905–41 it is an offence for any native to transfer South of the 20th parallel, except as permitted by the provision of this Section. For your information I am attaching a copy of this legislation. Under the circumstances Agnes will have to transfer to Beagle Bay and remain at that institution for the period of your absence from Derby or Broome.* Acting Commissioner of Native Affairs 20th November, 1946.

It was also reported to the Native Affairs Department that my father had met Mum at the jetty when the ship berthed at Broome on 3 December 1945. Mr King assured Native Affairs that Mum didn't know that Dad was waiting at the jetty and that it was only by virtue of Kathleen Scissors (Sesar), a sister of

Agnes, who had told Eusop bin Hussein that Agnes was coming by ship to Broome. Goodness sakes, they were sisters and their bonding was very strong so by our standards it was reasonable for Aunty Kudjie's action.

Mr King said that he had approached my father and in no uncertain terms said a few words to him. Mum was then bundled off to the convent without speaking to Dad. She was sent back to the mission by the mission truck, to wait there until the Kings' return to Derby for the next school year.

LITTLE MISSION GIRL

IT WAS A GOOD YEAR, THAT YEAR OF 1942. Maybe not for the world in the middle of its long and dismal journey into the bleakness of six painful years of war, but definitely for a small family in Beagle Bay. That was the year in which I was born and it was the beginning of over half a century of my living. I was now a colony kid, not by choice but circumstance. Putting it mildly, it was my destiny for I was meant to have been born in Moola Bulla. I have no misgivings about being born in my mimi's country and the old Beagle Bay people never let me forget the fact, either.

'You was a war baby. You was a war baby and don't you ever forget that. Don't you forget where you was born, too. This is your mimi's country.' That was all I ever heard when I was growing up. War babies must have been special, especially the ones born at Beagle Bay and there were quite a few, mind you.

I know that lots of loving arms held me dearly, shutting out the misery and cruelty of that horrible war. I had plenty of aunties and mimis to do that for me. They told me how I was so cute and cuddly, that I was chucked from one aunty to another and quite often my aunties would run away with me to the dormitories and keep me there overnight, hiding me from the mission Sisters. I know that I was a happy child, for that feeling of being loved and wanted by my family has been with me throughout my living memories. I know that it will stay with me forever.

While the other side of the world was in agony and turmoil, people had gone on with their daily routine at the mission as if they had no care in the world. Sure, everybody knew that there was a war going on, but it was so far away. That is, until 19th of February 1942, when the Japanese bombed Darwin, and then Broome a couple of weeks later. Those historic events made them sit up.

The Japanese were closer to home than the Germans, they told themselves and that made them more frightened than ever. With the influx of evacuees, the rumours got bigger and bigger by the minute. When the enemy landed, it was said, they'd take no prisoners and they'd behead all the people. My mob was a superstitious lot at the best of times and those rumours didn't help at all. That made them even more windy.

They were a bit fearful of the unknown, at least in their minds. My Mimi Alice and her mob had the fear and love of God in them all right but, believe me, the fear of the enemy soldiers on a rampage was even greater. Who could blame them? Mimi told me lots of stories when I became of listening age. That was only one of them and it was well after the war when she got around to telling it to me.

A favourite story about me was often told by my mum, Mimi Alice, Mimi Lena Cox, a cousin sister, and just about anyone else who knew about it. It was one of the days when they assumed Japanese planes were coming closer to the mission and everybody bolted. The sounds of the planes could be heard from a great distance, getting closer and closer by the minute. Again no one waited for the identification of the warplanes to be confirmed. They just headed for the bush. Except for me! My own mum and Mimi forgot all about poor little me! They left me for dead, it looked like. When Mum finally realised that she was without me, she ran back to the house only to find me gone.

She started shouting and yelling hysterically, 'Anyone seen little Betty-girl? She's gone! She's gone! Quick! Help me!'

By now the planes had passed over and there was no danger for the time being anyway.

But more panic now! Everybody had heard the news about me. People were running from house to house after hearing and seeing Mum gathering anyone in her wake to search for me. They looked in the nearby scrub, amongst the trees and under the brush. The old men even set their hunting dogs loose. Still there was no sign of me.

Kids were sent running to the convent and dormitories in case one of my aunties had taken me away to hide. No good there, either. About an hour later, someone discovered me with my *Lulu* David Cox, Mimi Lena's husband. He was cradling me in his arms under a shady tree and talking to me, his one wooden crutch lying beside him. In his younger days, Lulu David had lost his leg in an accident but managed very well with the one good leg, thus the wooden crutch.

Can you imagine this wonderful old man running away into the bush with a few-weeks-old baby in his arms, trying to get away from imminent danger? I certainly could because I grew up to know this fine old gentleman, just like my mimis.

When asked why he ran off with me, he answered, 'Well, everybody took off too quick. Somebody had to look after her. Them Japanese wasn't gonna get us. I don't know what happened to Aggie. She just took off with Alice and Lena. I heard little Betty-girl crying inside the house and just grabbed her. That's all. We just took off ourselves with fright.'

That story always made me feel happy and good inside. It still does. When I was smaller and knew the story off by heart, I'd ask my Mum, 'What kind that time with Lulu David during the war? I want to hear it again, please Mum?'

It was after the war when I left the mission but I can remember some of the events which must have occurred when I was about three or four years old, for I still see mind pictures of the ration drops from the Air Force planes. Everyone was running around like mad, headless chooks, running from drop to drop, untangling

26

the parachutes, dragging huge boxes and bags, chucking them into big heaps, ready for the mission truck to pick them up. Kids and dogs got tangled up in the mad rush. There was excitement all around, everybody getting in each other's way, big people and little people everywhere. We all knew that there must be good stuff in the boxes and bags because no one was allowed to touch the rations. Someone must have broken into a box, or it may have been broken on impact, because we were all handed out lollies, mainly barley sugar.

One of the most vivid memories of that time and the most delicious was the taste of barley sugar lollies in my mouth. Yes, barley sugar. Mmmm, I just loved that taste right from the very beginning. I don't know who gave them to me but I loved them because they had the strangest and sweetest taste ever. I tried so hard not to finish the barley sugar too quickly, because I wanted it to last forever. The only other sweet taste, apart from the rationed cane sugar, that I had ever tasted in my entire life was the *moonga* in the trees.

I grew up amongst women, mostly. There was my mother Agnes, Mimi Alice, my other mimis and my aunties Christina (Giggy), Bella and Philomena (Binyu). I remember them more clearly than the others because Aunties Betty, Kathleen (Kudjie) and Peggy (Peggo) had left the mission to seek work elsewhere or had gotten married. Aunty Kudjie had still been at the mission when I was born because she was my godmother and had left sometime afterwards to get married.

The story goes that my Christian name was supposed to be Patricia, having been born on the 17th of March, St Patrick's Day, but Aunty Kudjie changed it to Elizabeth, after my Aunty Betty who was living in Port Hedland with her husband Uncle Gerry Clarke. Mum just looked on in astonishment when Father Francis uttered the name Elizabeth in the ceremony. Mum had no choice in the matter. My poor godfather, Ambrose Cox (Uncle Umbood) was just as amazed because he knew that I was to be named Patricia. Those sisters had a special bond and we, their children, noticed it more and more as we grew older. Perhaps that's why Mum did not say anything but just let things be.

'You should have seen bublee Umbood's face, poor thing, but he had to go along with Kudjie,' Mum told the others later on at Mimi's house.

Uncle Umbood said that no one could tell Aunty anything, anyway. 'You know what kind Kudjie is. You gotta have a stand-up argument with her and then you'd lose, anyway,' he said.

Then of course, there was Cecilia, youngest of them all, who had been at the Holy Child Orphanage (HCO) in Broome since 1941 but moved to Beagle Bay when the orphanage relocated there during the war years. She was to become my aunty, sister, friend and littlest mum all rolled into one. That was the only way I could describe her when I later joined her at the orphanage in Broome.

Cecilia looked after me during all those lonely days and nights when my mum wasn't there for me. She was only about thirteen years old and already she had the task of being a mother to me. I hadn't realised then how lonely and painful her own childhood life must have been without her own mum, dad and sisters being with her. I believe that the longest time the sisters spent together was when Cecilia was a baby and then during the evacuation of Broome.

In 1936 when Lulu Willy Wright was sent to Derby to the

Leprosarium Hospital or 'Bungarun' as it was called, Mimi Alice left the mission to live in Broome. Although Cecilia was just two years old, she was to go with her.

There was a story about this regarding Lulu Gerome Manado, a cousin brother to Mimi Alice and full brother to Mimi Lena. He was out working on one of the mission's windmills when someone rode up and casually mentioned that he had just seen Alice getting ready to get on the mission truck with little Cecilia. The windmill would have been quite a few miles away from the mission but Lulu suddenly stopped work and saddled up his mule. Mules are stubborn by nature but that beast sure moved. They reckoned he looked like John Wayne at full gallop, speeding past the mission and full blast into the wind, whip going from side to side, urging the mule on. When he caught up with the truck it must have been about two miles away from the second gate. He stopped it and ordered Mimi and Cecilia off the truck.

'Alice, you're not going anywhere with Cissy. You know she's still too small and you're not flying around the countryside with her. Wait until she's a bit older than now. You hear?'

No way was Mimi going to get onto the mule and no way was she going to argue with her brother, so they walked slowly back to the mission with Aunty in the saddle. They laughed all the way back and so did everyone else when they heard the story.

The Holy Child Orphanage had opened in Broome in 1939 and according to the register of inmates, Cecilia entered on 26 April 1941. She left on 1 April 1949. Because of other circumstances surrounding their lives as well as the Native Protector's Act, the orphanage housed native girls who were either orphaned or had been taken there by the Native Affairs people.

Being brought up by women wasn't as traumatic as one might imagine. I quite enjoyed it. To me my aunties were beautiful young Nyul Nyul women with waist-long black hair, wavy and shining. They prided themselves with having luxurious hair and kept it plaited in long tresses, wound neatly around their heads and kept in place with hairpins and hair slides. My Aunty Binyu was the only one who had brown mousy hair, straight as pins and very unruly. No matter how many times her sisters tried to do her hair, it never stayed in place for too long. The girls on the mission helped each other to do their hair because nearly all of them grew their hair long and sometimes it was difficult to do their own. Quite often you'd see a few of them sitting in the sun outside the dorm, just combing and plaiting and chatting away like they had no trouble in the world. They took pride in themselves by their grooming and in later years the townspeople in Broome could tell they had mission upbringing.

I got to know all my aunties a lot better when they finally left the mission to live in Broome. They saw each other more often, with Aunty Betty coming for holidays from time to time, or the aunties going down to Port Hedland for short visits. As I grow

GIRLS' DORMITORIES, BEAGLE BAY, 1958

older I thank God that I knew them as my extra mums during their stay here on earth. I would have been truly lost without the closeness and support of my mothers, in Broome and Port Hedland. It was a feeling of belongingness.

On the mission, the married quarters where mums and dads raised their children was called the 'colony'. It was quite a distance away from the convent grounds and the girls' dormitories and about half a mile from the boys' dormitories where the Fathers and Brothers looked after them. The young colony children were taken from their parents when they were old enough to go to school. The little boys went to join the other boys and the little girls went to the convent. These children were taken away from home at about age five or six. After having lived in a sheltered environment with their families, they suddenly found themselves locked away from their very own home. For the next ten to twelve years they would have to be separated from their parents who only just lived over the fence. It must have been heartwrenching for those mums especially, to see their little babies taken from them, for they were just that, babies.

There were two dormitories for the girls, who were divided into age groups. My aunties lived in the big dorm with the other girls and older single women. Each dorm had one Sister to look after them. Because I was too young to live at the convent, my aunties would often sneak me into their dorm to sleep over with them. I think because they did not have a normal family upbringing, they threw their love on me and smothered me.

Whenever Mum or Mimi Alice came to the fence to visit, my aunties would carry me to their dorm and send a message back to say that they were keeping me there for the night. Once inside they'd hide me under the bed until the Sister did her rounds. Being the youngest of the three, Aunty Binyu had to keep an eye out for Sister in case she caught us out and sent me back. I was told to keep quiet or *jujud* would get me. I was more scared of jujud than of Sister. I didn't want to live with any old devil, thank you very much. So I stayed put. When the coast was clear I'd crawl out from underneath and climb onto the bed.

I could never understand the logic of my family when I was young. Here was my mum and Mimi telling me to be brave and not to fear the dark because there was no jujud there, then there were my aunties scaring the living daylights out of me, telling me that the jujud was out there to grab me any time I misbehaved.

I was one spoilt child though. My aunties played all kinds of games with me nearly all night long, trying to make me talk, laugh and sing, until I dropped down in sheer exhaustion and fell into deep sleep. The other girls would often join in the fun and games. They must have missed their little brothers and sisters, too. You see, a lot of them came from other parts of the Kimberley such as the Halls Creek and Wyndham areas. They were miles and miles away from their homes. Sister must have been a heavy sleeper because she never came to check on the noise.

Most of the girls smoked tailor-made cigarettes, sneaked in by somebody, of course. Like a big shot I'd have a puff with them, choking and spluttering, making everybody laugh themselves silly. I thought it was really great making them laugh that way. 'Oh good!' I thought to myself. 'I'll do it again and make them laugh some more.' I'd feel so sick and groggy after some more puffs but I still wanted to hear them laugh out more. Besides the smoking, some of the girls learned to chew stick tobacco as well. Aunty Giggy was one of them and still chewed *moolidjin* when she was an old lady. Lots of times she'd try to teach me how to 'cook' the moolidjin with the *goonoor* tree *gujud*. I always declined because I never liked the smell of the tobacco and gujud when it was wet. Thankfully, I did not take up either habit.

Early in the morning, when Sister unlocked the door, Aunty Giggy would sneak me out to the shower block for a quick shower. She'd comb my long black hair, which was thick and curly, tying it with strips of pretty material that she saved from the sewing classes. Other times she'd simply make ringlets. She said she just loved to 'pretty me up'.

Aunty later became an excellent seamstress when she moved to town and had a good reputation. She sewed such beautiful frocks for a lot of the ladies of Broome for weddings and everyday wear. She didn't use shop-bought dress patterns, just using the skills of measurements that the nuns taught her. She even tried her hand at tailoring, making men's and boy's trousers.

Much, much later my lovely aunty became a victim of Moola Bulla Station in the East Kimberley where law-breakers from throughout the Kimberley were sent. One time she was slightly intoxicated walking home but that was good enough for the law to nab her. Her little son Billy Boy went with her to that lonely place. We cried for them for a long time. She returned to Broome with her husband Uncle Allan Turner and a new addition to her family many years later. We surely had missed her and Billy Boy.

Mum waited for me by the fence each morning after the dormitory sleepovers. Sometimes, when walking back to the colony, I'd ask her questions. I'd often wonder why my aunties did not live with us at home, so I'd ask her about it.

Mum said, 'When you get older you'll know all about it. Don't ask me stupid things right now.'

I wanted to know right there and then, not later on when I'd be old and grey! I can't remember whether she eventually told me herself, or whether somebody else did. Whichever way I found out still bothered me, because I just couldn't understand why they couldn't be with us at home. I wanted them around me all the time and to live with us. For all my questioning nature I never really asked about my father. I just took it for granted that he was in Broome waiting for us and that we'd be together again one day.

THE GARDEN
OF EDEN

JUST ABOUT EVERY DAY WAS A BEAUTIFUL DAY.
Every tree and blade of grass was so green and lush. They were
sun-filled days, with the smell of ti-trees and smoke clinging
to the cool morning air with the birds and leret making music
in the bush, loud enough but not too noisy for our little ears,
simply beautiful. There were the sounds of people waking up
and coming to life for yet another day. They were mission people
getting ready to go to work, some going to early Mass before
work with wives joining them, carrying their babies in their arms.
They were mission people just being mission people.

At the back of the convent and dorm areas stood the enormous
garden fields where just about everything grew. Rows and rows of
different vegetables and patches of different varieties of melons
and beans, all shades of green. There were also sweet potatoes,
corn and leek. You name it and it was there. It was as close to a
miniature Garden of Eden on earth. I thought it was, anyway.

While the big people worked away in the sun, my friends and
cousins played amongst the banana palms and coconut palms,
pinching ripe tomatoes, snake beans and whatever else was ready
for eating. They smelled so good and so earthily fresh. Sometimes
I'd just grab a handful of moist dirt, bring it up to close to my
nose and smell it, breathing in deeply, exhaling slowly and trying
to prolong the scent of nature. It was so peaceful and cool in the
garden. I'd go there whenever I could, any chance I'd get.

There was a big shed down the bottom of the garden where
old Brother Mathias worked. Actually, there were two gardens
at the mission, the other being Brother John's. The gardens were
named after the two Brothers so that the workers knew in which
garden to work for the day. Some of the garden hands said that
old Brother Mathias even slept there because that was his garden
kingdom. He loved the place so dearly. Sometimes and only

sometimes, he'd call us over to give us a taste of watermelon or rockmelon or whatever. Both Brothers had a huge responsibility in keeping the mission supplied with fruit and vegetables, especially during wartime with rationing and short supplies of goods. They had a job to do all right. Things were sure tough on everybody during those times.

I followed my aunties everywhere, even down to the freshwater springs, looking for edible plant and fruit and if they were lucky enough, finding moonga. They taught me to eat the waterlily plant, which I didn't like. at all

Aunty Bella told me, 'Don't worry about the taste. Just eat it. You'll get used to it. If you get lost in the bush and get hungry, what you gonna eat, hey?'

'But this got no taste,' I insisted. She didn't take any notice of me but called out, 'Binyu! You better take this girl and tell her properly about things. She's gotta learn something about bush tucker. If you don't do it, I'll tell Aggie on you. You hear?'

With that she went on looking for some more bush tucker and left me with Aunty Binyu.

FRESHWATER SPRING AT BEAGLE BAY, 1958

The old people used to say that if ever you got lost and thirsty, you could just dig a hole in the ground around Beagle Bay and water would come gushing up through the sand. They were always talking about things like that. If you got caught in a storm, never stand under trees, for lightning strikes trees more than they strike people. I was fascinated with those stories but they didn't mean much to me at that time, in one ear and out the other. I wish I had taken more notice then, but I was only a kid.

On some days, I guess they must have been Saturdays or Sundays, families went fishing or hunting or gathering bush tucker. Some went for walks in the bush to teach the children about their Aboriginal ways, legends of the area and about how our people used to live, a long, long time ago. The old people used to sing to us in language and tell us about the land, the animals, birds and the sea creatures in story form. Our mimis also tried to teach us little ones to talk in language.

Our mimis spoke several languages because of the different language groups in the Nyul Nyul country. My mum's age group would probably have been one of the last to have heard or spoken fluent language at home.

I only learned the names of animals, birds and fish as well as the body parts, just enough to get by but that was forgotten when I went to Broome, because nobody spoke it there, I suppose. Until the day she died, Mimi Alice never forgot Nyul Nyul and she still spoke it when she caught up with her Beagle Bay families. Most of us school kids just spoke English and really, nobody seemed to carry on the language. It was being lost to us even then.

Whenever I asked Mum whether she still knew our language,

she'd reply, 'Only a little bit and what you gotta ask so many questions for, anyway?' She didn't seem to want to talk about it. It was probably painful to talk about such matters.

Sadly our language was not encouraged at the mission. The really old people who were there when the missionaries arrived still spoke their language and carried out their law regardless of the missionaries' occupation of their land. In time though, I suppose they and their children became baptised in the Catholic faith and slowly their ways became lost.

I am sure that the old people would have tried very hard to keep alive everything traditional and sacred to their way of life. It was their way to do whatever they could to keep the culture alive in the children, even if only by doing it in secret. It is so sad that time was against them because the next generation was slowly losing its culture.

The fishing spots were quite a distance away, sometimes miles and miles away but no worries for that mob. They'd just pack up and go: kids and dogs, the young and the old, anyone who was able to walk because walking for miles was no big deal to them. Once their minds were made up, they'd just go, go, go! You fellas not leaving us behind, they'd say.

On one such occasion, my third birthday to be exact, the family took me with them as a birthday treat. I knew we had a long way to walk so I begged to be carried.

'Please, Uncle. Gimmee *goondoo*. Gimmee goondoo. I feel slack,' I cried. Aunty Bella told me that I used to talk that way to my uncles, the Cox brothers, Mimi Lena's sons. So up on their shoulders I'd go, clapping with glee. It was better than piggyback rides or hip carrying. Smaller babies were carried in *bindjins* by their mums or mimis.

Everyone went crabbing or fishing. Like any nosy kid I

followed my uncles, making sure I was not too close otherwise they'd send me back so I started copying their actions from a distance, poking sticks into mud holes, trying to see if there were any crabs in them. All of a sudden I threw the stick away and stuck my hand inside the hole. Next minute I let out an unholy scream, yelling, crying and jumping about all at the same time, trying to shake off a big mangrove crab from my fingers. It had a really good grip of my fingers with its mighty claws. Everyone came running back to see what was happening. Finally, someone prised open the claws and freed my poor little fingers. I found out later that it was Uncle Mathew Cox who helped me. They made a big fuss over me after that, even though they were killing themselves laughing. To this day the remaining family members still remind me of that fateful day and laugh about it.

While the others fished, the older kids gathered wood for the fire. It was usually the older women who started the fire in readiness for the crabs, fish, shellfish and sometimes oysters in the shell. Billycan tea was made and if the women did not bring damper from home, they'd make some out there. If the men got lucky in hunting, there'd also be kangaroo or *barney* to cook. If some people didn't have a very good day catching fish or anything, the others shared their good fortune with them, making sure that everyone had a good feed.

Later on, someone would bring out a tin of treacle or some moonga to spread on the damper. I loved dipping the damper into the pannikin of tea. The pannikins were made from used jam tins and fruit tins and fashioned with handles. Every pannikin was treasured dearly, for the tins were hard to come by. They all knew which pannikin belonged to whom, even though they all looked the same to me.

The only trouble with picnics was the long trek back home.

Anyway, I didn't have to worry, I'd be carried back home by one of my uncles. I'd be so tired I couldn't remember being bathed in the oval-shaped tin washtub, until the next morning when I'd wake up in a clean cotton nightie.

KIMBERLEY KIDS

MANY OF THE KIDS LIVING ON THE MISSION were from the Kimberley or down south. I don't know how often the 'human round-ups' took place but it must have been several times in a year. It would have been both frightening and horrifying to the people and their children, families being torn apart, separated and taken by force by the government people. Most were just babes in the bush. Some of them were still sucking on their mother's *nyanyas*!

All those children were subjected to the so-called Native Protection Policy and forcibly removed from their families to assimilate in white man's society. The theory was that, in three generations or so, the half-caste and quarter-caste children would be bred out and the Aboriginal problem would no longer exist.

While many white people believed that Aboriginal mothers rejected their part-Aboriginal children and were ready to give them away, it simply was not the case. Wherever people of different races associated with each other there were bound to be children of mixed races born to them. Sometimes they were raised by both parents, who sought permission to marry by being granted a Certificate of Exemption or Citizenship Rights but more often they were raised by the Aboriginal mother.

Perhaps those children of lighter or pale skin may have been frowned upon by the full blood people at first but they were accepted, loved and followed the law of their Aboriginal ancestors until that world came to an end by their forced removal. Even to this day, one can still see light-skinned children and adults right there amongst their people. These groups of Aboriginal people have continuous ties with their ancestral lands, and the men still take the young boys through the Law and teach them men's business.

This country has a long history in placing children, especially those who came from the settlers and who were poor, neglected or had delinquent tendencies, into institutions, orphanages or foster homes.

Around the mission I noticed that the people had different skin tones. Some were fair, almost like white people, some were shades of brown, while others were very dark or black. Every time I asked how come some of them were different colours, I was told the same things as before.

'You'll know when you get older! Be patient! Can't you stop quiet for a change! Somebody, take this child away from me!'

So I kept on playing with the children of 'different coloured skins' still wondering, still getting no answers. Of course, I did find out when I got older. I thought, 'Ah ha, now I know why.'

There were a few children from other Kimberley areas who came from the same camps or tribal areas and who knew each other. Many were too young to know where they came from and could remember only a little about their former lives when they were older. Then there were children who were old enough and lucky enough to be able to tell others to whom they belonged and from where they came. This proved helpful when it came to the marriage law, knowing they did not marry the wrong way or wrong skin. Perhaps some did cross the line, unknowingly. One will never know, for it could quite easily have happened all those years ago. It happened not only in Western Australia but all over Australia, wherever the displaced and dispossessed Aboriginals were taken.

For the lost memories and lost years of our people, who were once children, I feel so very sad about that part of our history. The government of that time may have thought that it was doing the right thing by Aboriginal people but it proved almost fatal and certainly destructive for our race.

My Lulu Willy Wright came from Turkey Creek but was old enough and fortunate enough to remember the little ones who were taken away from his mob. Even though he must have only been about ten or twelve years old, he told them who he was, told each one how they were related and from which country they came. He and the older boys and girls kept that knowledge alive in themselves throughout all those years, so that one day they could go back to their country and find their people who would have been in perpetual mourning. God willing, their mums and dads would still be alive and well. Those were the kinds of hope which kept them going, for without hope they would have perished spiritually.

None of the Aboriginal women would have willingly given up her child or children so easily, especially in those times. I can only imagine the mournful wailing that would have gone on and on, those mothers throwing themselves on the ground, rolling around and hitting themselves on their heads until they bled and were totally exhausted. There was endless pain for them and they would have carried it right through until they died.

Lulu didn't talk much but he told me that the troopers in the Kimberley were supposed to round up the half-caste and quarter-caste kids in the camps or stations. If they happened to capture full blood kids, they too were sent to the mission because they didn't really care who were sent there. It was the part-white children who were the main target for they had to be 'saved' from that pagan lifestyle of Aboriginal people and groomed in the white man's way of life.

When word got around that the troopers were coming, the mothers tried to hide their fair-skinned children by painting them with charcoal mixture to blend in with the rest of them. They also tried to hide them further into the scrub or caves. Painting

Lulu Willy and hiding him worked for a good many years but he was finally captured and brought to the mission. George Wright had wanted to bring his son to Beagle Bay himself but instead Lulu was put on a ship in Wyndham Port with other kids.

There were plenty of stories about children being transported to Wyndham Port by bullock carts and then shipped to Broome for Beagle Bay by lugger or truck. Four and five year olds, younger ones as well, were put on the big ships, crying day and night for their mothers and families. The smaller ones were starving themselves out of sheer terror of the white people because the older ones told them that the whitefella's tucker might be poisoned and they'd die without seeing their families again. Well, some of them nearly did starve themselves to death! No way were they going to eat the strange food and drinks! On top of that they had never seen the seemingly endless ocean in their little lives, let alone travelling by sea. The rolling of the ships sent tremors through their bodies. They were terrified. They only knew the rivers and billabongs after the rains, not this endless expanse of the ocean.

Two of those little girls were Aunty Bella Lynot and her younger sister Aunty Barb, mother of Pearl and Sally. They were only about five and seven years old in the early 1900s but they remembered those times of fear and of the unknown. They were Lulu's people, his nieces.

Years down the track Aunty Bella became the head caregiver at the Holy Child Orphanage for girls in Broome. Although she had never married, she was mother to all the Kimberley kids and they never forgot her. When HCO closed she went to live with her sister Barb.

Those white protectors didn't have an ounce of understanding about the cultural needs and behaviour of those children, whose fate was at stake in a totally strange environment. They were away from their traditional land and would have been culturally uneasy. Some of the stolen children may have been dispossessed of their country but were strong in spirit and character. There were others who were mentally destroyed and never recovered. They needed help then and still do now.

Older children tried to keep their languages and customs alive by talking to each other when no one else was around and by telling stories and anything of importance to their traditions and beliefs. That may have gone on for a while but along the way there was bound to be a breakdown in their efforts, for there were no elders from their country to continue the teachings of their ancestors or to guide them into adulthood. There was only so much that a child could do. They could only teach up to their own level of knowledge and ability. They could go no further than themselves. Their cut-off point in learning and teaching was when they were removed.

Eventually, they forgot what they knew of their language and traditional ways and time slowly suffocated their memories. Over

MISSION BOYS PLAYING, 1950s

47

a period of time, those children began to speak a little of the local language of the Nyul Nyul people, as well as English and a little bit of German, with a hint of Irish. Sadly enough the entire Nyul Nyul language couldn't be fully saved. Today, there are greater efforts being made to retrieve lost languages of the Indigenous people of our country, and to trace family history. Perhaps this is too late in many areas.

Is it any wonder when people say that we have a strange way of talking? That Broome talk, they say. Being brought up with our own native language, German, Irish, Spanish and Australian English, what could one expect?

MISSION
LIFE

THE MISSION BUILDINGS WERE BUILT through Aboriginal labour and the expertise of the missionaries. From 1891 the Trappist Order ran the Mission, and in the early 1900s they handed over to the Pallottine Society. The arrival of the St John of God Sisters in 1907 contributed to the education of the children and the nursing of the whole community. They were qualified in both areas and nursing, especially, was most needed in the remote outback. The missionaries taught the young boys and men trade skills in carpentry, farming and butchering as well as mechanics and driving the vehicles around the mission. The girls and women were taught sewing, cooking and laundry work as well as baby care for the young mothers and mothers-to-be. Later on music and art played a great part in their education. They read music as well as playing by ear.

In turn the men helped build their own houses and other dwellings, such as the church, which were made from local stone and mortar. Shell grit was carted from the beaches many, many miles away. In summer the houses were cool and in the colder months they were warm, especially with the open fireplace being kept lit at night. It could get really cold there and most mornings the buckets of water turned into ice.

The houses were simple in construction with a large main room, enclosed verandahs (added later on), cooking and eating areas, and an outhouse down the back. The design was basic but it was adequate for their needs and cyclone-safe from the tropical weather. The people did not think of their houses as being their greatest possession but only as shelters from the environment and a gathering place for their families, extended relations, friends and countrymen.

Traditional people built their shelters or 'homes' from the environment around them for temporary use, but dismantled them for they knew that everything goes back into the environment. They could rebuild next time they moved camp.

The houses were built close to one another and loud exchanges of greetings and gossip were common. Even family rows and disagreements were morning topics, but that was normal. There was hustle and bustle every morning, fires being stoked up, pots and pans being rattled, the aroma of hot tea, coffee and warm goat's milk pungent in the cool, crisp air.

Mullamulla-eyed and *goonbi*-nosed kids played near the single hand-pumped underground well, which supplied the colony with fresh drinking water. Men and women carried buckets of water as there was no running water from taps in the houses.

The men had their jobs to do, each going to their own work place, whether it was the bakery, gardens or checking the windmills. The women stayed at home to look after the babies and little ones, or worked elsewhere for a few hours. Some helped out at the church, convent, presbytery or the Brothers' houses. There was no such thing as idle hands. They all knew their jobs and did them well.

Their lives were structured and organised for them. As long as they lived their lives in that order, they'd be living the 'right' way. They wouldn't be living the 'pagan' lifestyle that their people had supposedly lived for centuries. Our people were shown how to live an orderly lifestyle and in that short time they learned to conform.

The people on the mission, my own mob and others, were happy in their own way, I suppose, doing what was expected of them, but I wonder how many of them longed for their ancestors' way of life: that way of life denied to them.

BEAGLE BAY CHURCH, 1958

So organised were their lives that the whole mission community were ordered or summoned by the bell. The bell woke them in the morning, drew them to church, told them when to start work, when to stop, when to eat and when to sleep. We all lived by the bell, including me at that tender age. Such a wonderful, big loud bell it was! It made me a little bit conscious of time but I'm afraid that I never lived in a time frame of any sort. Time never really meant that much to me when I was little, only such times when I was hungry, then I knew it was time to eat, or that the picture-show started at eight o'clock and I'd better get moving otherwise I'd miss the start. Things like that.

When I was older and went to boarding school at St Brigid's College, Lesmurdie, I had to train myself to be more time conscious, because it got me into a lot of hot water. I was always ten minutes behind play, always the last one in line or at the dining table. Because I was forever late for Mass, I was usually fixing my stockings in the chapel when everyone was bowed in prayer. I had to live in a white man's world and it was hard work.

I really did try because when it came to exams I made sure the tests were completed in time. This small time resolution made me conscious of the changes I had to make.

Going back to the bell, I'd like to tell you a little more of the powers of that bell and the order of everyday living on the mission. At every noon, the bell rang and everybody stopped dead in their tracks. I mean everybody. That was Angelus time and the whole mission knew it. They dropped everything to say the Angelus. The people could be out in the fields, or hanging out the clothes, or just having a drink of water at the well. They'd just stop, drop, kneel, bless themselves and pray. All over the place you could hear the chant '…The Angel of the Lord declared unto Mary…And she conceived of the Holy Ghost…Hail Mary full of Grace.' It was so beautiful to see and hear the people pray. It wasn't a put-on act either; it was the reverence and respect of the teachings of the Church that was implanted in them and passed on to their children.

My aunties came over to see us down at the colony on Sundays and Holy Days of Obligation or church holidays. Otherwise they waited anxiously and hopefully along the fence after suppertime of a night, even if just to get a glimpse of us. It was very rarely that families didn't go to the fence to see their children. The dormitory boys also came along the fence but kept to the boys' side under close supervision of the Brothers or Fathers. All along the fence, everybody exchanged news, brought spare tucker, sometimes cooked kangaroo meat and tails, emu, fish, billycan tea and damper. They brought whatever they had, which wasn't too much but which was really appreciated by everyone.

The dividing fence looked like stockyard fencing that kept horses and bullocks at bay. This fence separated the families and children as well as the missionaries. There were always a nun and priest on hand, walking the length and breadth of the grounds, silently keeping vigil, by reciting the rosary over and over, until visiting time was up. Young men and women of marriageable age did their courting under strict supervision, hence the evening vigil. Couples in love paired off further down the fence, their courtship done over the dividing line. That was how it went on for years and years, long after I left the mission. That was the proper way they were told.

We all knew that the stockyard fence was the boundary line. No one crossed it unless permission was given or some daredevils sneaked over. There were a few dobbers-in and the daredevils would always cop it. I had watched a few 'payback' fights, with little girls shouting, 'Knocks go, Sister! Knocks go, Sister! Big fight! Big fight! Hurry up!' Sister would come running to break up the fight, pulling the girls apart or clipping their ears.

BEAGLE BAY MISSION PLAYING FIELD, 1958

There was a huge playing field between the colony and the convent where the boys and girls played at recess or weekends. One day Aunty Binyu was playing rounders and on the run home she slid and cut her leg on a broken glass. Blood was spurting everywhere, girls screaming for Sister, little ones running backwards and forwards to their mums, telling them what had happened. Panic! Women came running out of their houses, either yelling out to one another or to nobody in particular, asking what was happening or who was hurt. It was so easy for the women to get excited.

'Binyu! It's Binyu! Someone get jidja Alice! Someone get Aggie! Hurry up!' Those cries soon got everybody to the scene.

Sister Therese finally came and tied a tourniquet around her leg and asked the big boys to carry her to the clinic, where her leg was promptly stitched up. Sister did a really fine job on her leg and the wound healed up with no infection. Many years afterwards I could still run my fingers along that scar, remembering very clearly about that day. Aunty said that I must have a very fine memory for it was such a long time ago.

I said to her, 'You know what, Aunty? I'm glad you don't hurt anymore but that scar still looks like a big centipede to me.'

My aunties were very protective towards me, especially Aunty Binyu. Heaven help anyone who teased me or made me cry! She was so unpredictable, too. You'd never know what she'd do. She was likely to go right up to that person and knock her flat! She could never stop still, always fidgety, always playing tricks on people, old and young. Too lively! Too jumpy! No one could really get angry with her, for that was the kind of girl she was, always doing silly things and making everyone laugh. She could drive anyone up the wall with her antics. Mimi Alice could only wring her hands in anguish. She often said to Mum, 'I don't know what to do with that girl. Thank God the Sisters have her now. They can look after her just as well as I can. She might be better off with her other sisters there. I can have a good spell for a change. Maybe if your father was here he might straighten her out.'

One time when we all lived under the same roof, down the marsh, my mum asked her to go to the shop.

'Binyu, can you go to Mr Tack's and get me one App-la-day? Come straight back, too.'

(Hardly anyone spoke in exact terms. It was always one of this or one of that, not one packet of cigarettes but one cigarette, meaning one packet of cigarettes. It was short-cut talk.)

So when she came back she threw Mum a big red apple and said, 'Here Aggie, catch!'

'What's this for, Binyu?'

'That's the apple you wanted. You said you wanted one apple a day.'

She was grinning from ear to ear, thinking that she had done a good job. Mum was lost for words.

'You can just take that back to Mr Tack and I'll write you a note this time, hear that? I said App-la-day, the tablets, not one apple. What am I gonna do with one apple when we've got the biggest mob in the house, hey? You must be cracked all right.'

So she ran all the way back to Tack's store, not caring a wink. No one could ever really get angry with Aunty Binyu.

I just loved rainy days at Beagle Bay. Sometimes it would rain for days and days, causing the gullies to fill, creating *wurumbas* to run, thus letting us swim in the swift running waters.

My aunties held me tightly to them, in case the current swept me away. I loved clinging to them, screaming and laughing at the same time. I knew that they would never let me go. I knew that I was safe in their arms.

Soon after the rains came, the croaking frogs lifted their voices in earnest revelry, in appreciation of the rains. It made me really sick in the head listening to them, all day and all night. They never seemed to give up. They hopped and jumped all over the place, sometimes getting accidentally squashed underfoot. That would make me jump too because I wore no shoes and it felt so yucky. I didn't mind playing with the smaller frogs though but when there was an over abundance of them, it was sickening to my stomach. When the colony kids got together, after being so bored at home, we'd wander into the convent grounds to play under the big trees that stood between the convent and the church.

We'd begin looking for the frogs in the damp ground or under the oleander trees. Sometimes we'd dig around looking for the gobble-gobble frogs. They were nice, small sand frogs and easy to handle. It was funny watching the gobble-gobbles wriggling their way into the damp sand. Sometimes I'd stop their wriggling

BEAGLE BAY CHURCH, 1958

progress halfway by placing my fingers at the back of them, just to watch them start all over again. Poor little frogs! None of us had dolls to play with so I suppose the next best thing was playing with the live baby frogs.

We liked going to the church because there'd be frogs lying in wait for us in the holy water founts beside the doors. Big green ones! We all knew that the frogs were there but every time we went to bless ourselves with the holy water, we'd pretend that they weren't there, so that we could let out a big yell. It was one kid after another yelling or screaming. Every time we touched the frogs we'd laugh our little heads off, in the church, mind you. It was a place of God and worship. If our parents or mimis knew what we were doing, there'd be punishment for us for sure.

I especially liked to play with the pale beige, slender-looking frogs that we called 'Our Lady' frogs. Today, the white chocolate Freddos remind me of those frogs. I detested the big, ugly dark greeny-black ones. I used to think that they were poisonous for they seemed to live in the poisonous oleander trees. I called them the 'devil' frogs because they looked so evil.

There were days when we'd just go into the church to pray and feel holy. None of us knew how to say the prayers properly but we tried anyway. When someone said a prayer that sounded wrong, we'd all pipe up saying, 'Ah ha, wrong! Not like that! Like this!' If we genuflected on the wrong knee or blessed ourselves back to front, we'd chant, 'Ah ha, sin! Ah ha, sin!' not really knowing what sin was, only that it must have been something bad. Sometimes we'd go into the confessional box and pretend to confess, copying the grown-ups. Again, we didn't know what sin was but we just yarned away and laughed like kids do. It sure made us feel holy going to church though, gazing in awe at the statues, especially the Virgin Mary and Jesus on the Crucifix.

The altar always fascinated us. It was so beautiful. It was decorated with pearl shells and the mother-of-pearl was intricately worked into the timber and marble-like altar. We were told our grandparents helped build the church and that my Mimi Alice and Rosie Wiley painted the two angels on the wall.

No matter at what angle I looked at the statues, it appeared as if their gazes were following me around. I felt great.

'Look you fellas, Jesus is looking at me,' I called out.

'Not even. You come over here and watch Him. He's looking at us over here, not at you,' the others replied.

We all insisted He was looking at us in that special way. Whenever any of us were naughty, we'd remind each other that we'd better behave, or else! We'd better look out for those eyes, they see everything and know everything. Our parents told us the same things, that God was watching and we'd better be good or jujud would grab us and drag us to hell to live with him. We were frightened of jujud, all right.

Washing days at the convent were really something to watch. The coppers were lit early in the morning, ready for the boiling of the clothes. There were mountains and mountains of clothes to be washed. There were no washing machines, only rows of troughs with scrubbing boards in them. Those young washerwomen were a sight to see. They'd just scrub, scrub, scrub, making hand washing look so easy. It was non-stop going, only pausing briefly to wipe their foreheads or have a drink of water. If any of them got tired, there was always another one to take her place. While the young women and girls washed at the troughs or large tin tubs, others carried the clothes to the boiling coppers, poking the

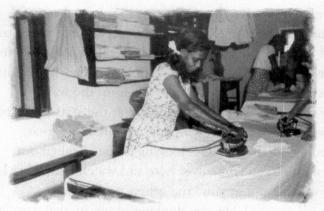

DOMESTIC DUTIES, BEAGLE BAY, 1950s

clothes down with the long copper sticks, until they were ready to be taken out and put in the rinsing tubs to be wrung out and finally hung on the lines. While all this work was going on, that didn't stop the laughing and carrying on amongst the girls.

The bright white, billowing habits of the Sisters looked like clouds in the sky, flapping in the breeze, high on the lines, stretching endlessly, or so it seemed. On top of the Sisters' laundry, they had to launder the Brothers' and Fathers' habits and clothes. There were sheets and towels, altar linen and vestments, the lot. Washing days were part and parcel of their everyday work.

Sometimes I'd watch in fascination at the young women and girls who ironed the habits and clothes of the religious. Not so much at the clothes but at the way in which they wielded the flat-irons, expertly flattening the pleats of the cumbersome habits, making each pressing movement of the iron, a real work of art. They had to be fast as well, for the irons lost heat very quickly and they had to keep swapping the irons around on top of the stove tops. They had to make sure the clothes did not get scorched because of the uncontrolled heating of the irons.

Perspiration just flowed freely from their faces and bodies. My poor aunties! To think that in years down the track, there'd be automatic washing machines, dryers and boy, oh, boy, automatic steam irons and clothes pressers. Regardless of what the future held in store, they still laundered the clothes spotlessly with the out-dated appliances left over from my Mimi's days.

What a wonderful innocent childhood we had on the mission. It was great being that age, too young to be in the convent and too small to work. We had our own kind of freedom, playing around places which were forbidden to others, finding out about insects, butterflies and flowers, what made things grow and why they withered and died. They were mysterious to us but it never stopped us from wondering about nature. It was an early education, with us being both teachers and pupils. We were finding out things for ourselves, by asking questions, not fully understanding the answers but still being satisfied with them.

I learned that plants needed the sun and rain for them to grow and for the fruit to ripen. I knew that the goats had to be milked otherwise their nyanyas would get swollen and they'd be in pain. I knew that if the March flies' wings were pulled, they wouldn't be able to fly and would die. We learned things our own way.

Sometimes our little gang would go into the surrounding bush to look for bush fruit, moonga or other bush tucker but weren't successful. Our mimis showed us what fruit and plants to eat, what not to eat, the poisonous ones and medicinal ones. They told us stories along the way, true ones and legends of the area, funny ones and sad ones. They tried to tell us about surviving in the bush but we were too young to understand and take them all in, but I remember some stories about children and people getting lost, being found dead or not at all.

Now that I am older and a little wiser, I often reflect on the things our mimis told us. Their teachings began centuries ago, long before they were born. That was the way our customs and traditions were handed down. They had no pens and paper to record any events and stories to tell their children and to others, so storytelling and dancing were the only way they knew how to relay their history. I wish I had taken more notice of my mimis and listened more closely to their teachings and stories.

Outside the colony boundary lived my old mimis and lulus and other old people who lived their traditional ways. They lived in the camps with their dogs and dingo pups, cooking in the open, sitting down all day under the tree shade, chewing their moolidjin, the half blind leading the blind to go from one camp to the other, visiting their own mob to yarn. They didn't care that perhaps their children and their grandchildren, through no fault of their own, were living the whitefellas' style and maybe getting a little too flash. They accepted the missionaries for what they were but they were too set in their ways to truly conform to the new ways, even though they had converted to Christianity. Their culture could not be driven out of them. It was good enough that their children were changing and learning the new ways, so they were left to live out their traditional life style in peace, until they passed on. The missionaries still had an obligation to care for them, though, health wise and food wise, as well as spiritually.

I'd visit them with Mimi Alice and Mimi Lena quite regularly, the two old girls bringing them *mayi* and billycan tea. The old people in the camps were never forgotten by their own mob. They got their ration quota every week but they were too old to hunt and gather, so the extra food really came in handy for them. They looked forward to any bush tucker and meat that others brought to share with them.

I remember old Mimi Fanny quite well. When I was small, I was told that she was Mimi Alice's mother but Mimi's birth mother was Maudie who had died. For years I truly believed that she was the birth mother, not fully understanding the significance of Aboriginal kinship, the very closeness and togetherness of family life, the basis of the extended family system. This extended family system reached beyond the horizon until our fingertips touched the other side. That's the only way I can describe it.

Out of all the mimis in the camp, I loved Mimi Fanny the best. She was a full-blooded Aboriginal woman, old and grey but was quite fit for her age. She was said to have been very strong and a good fighting woman. She spoke a little English but spoke mostly in language to us.

On one particular outing with my mimis, I happened to look up towards the sky and suddenly something caught my eyes.

'Look up there, Mimi! Something's there!' I cried, tugging at Mimi Alice's skirt. Before I knew it, I was pulled along so quickly that I nearly stumbled and fell over a couple of times.

'Don't look! Don't look! Something might grab us!' she said. Close behind us Mimi Lena and a couple of the other old girls were moving at the same pace as us, blessing themselves and praying, 'Holy Mother of God, pray for us. Come on, hurry up.'

A short distance further on we all stopped, puffed out and breathing heavily. After we caught our breaths, I was told that what I saw was an old 'burial' tree. I didn't have a clue what a burial tree was. I thought that burial was when the dead were put into the ground, prayers were said and they were covered over with dirt and everybody crying. I went to a few funerals on the mission, even though I was only a kid but that was all I knew about burials. Apparently in the old days, it was customary to 'bury' the dead in that way and some of the old people still wanted to be buried like that, even after the missionaries had firmly established themselves out there. They had said that the whitefellas had strange ways and that they could keep their strangeness to themselves.

My mimis never told me the full story of the burial tree, so I guess I'll never ever know now. Anyway, they probably would have told me to wait until I was older, as usual.

We went back to the colony laden with bush tucker and had a good feed afterwards, sharing with the others. No matter who had the most bush tucker or who caught the most fish or meat, they were always shared, even if only a morsel each.

After lunch or dinner time, as it was called, the girls had to have a rest. The big girls went to the big dorm and the little girls to the little dorm. The same applied to the boys. The girls were locked in by Sister, then she went to the convent to have her rest or whatever else that nuns do in their quiet time. There was always someone older who took charge of the dorm while Sister was away. Aunty Imelda was in charge of the little dorm and had charge of the keys. She was a relation of ours, so it was okay with us because she often let my aunties take me to the big dorm. Sometimes Aunty Binyu would ask Sister if I could have rest time with them and jidja Aggie could pick me up. Because I was a good girl, Sister often gave in to her. The afternoon rest probably had different rules than night time, for there was little fuss towards teeny ones having rest with their aunties or sisters.

After the girls were locked inside, they could either go to sleep or do the things they wanted to do so long as they did not make too much noise. They were on their honour. They would read books, write letters, sew or do their hair: combing, brushing, braiding or cutting each other's hair. I'd watch for hours at the girls combing their hair into rolls or pinning them up with hairpins and hairslides, making them into buns, French rolls or ringlets. These girls treasured every comb, brush, hairpin, hairslide, ribbon, mirror, soap, powder or whatever they happened to own. I know my aunties loved their 'Lifebuoy' and 'Pears' soaps, 'Evening in Paris' scent, as well as the 'Three Flowers' hair oil. They loved to dust themselves down with 'Johnson's Baby Powder' and when I used it on my own babies, I always thought of them.

The same went for sewing needles and cotton, safety pins and hankies. They even treasured broken fragments of mirror, calling them their 'looking glass'. Those little 'luxuries' were usually presents from families living outside the mission, in Broome or Derby, sending them with the mission truck driver. I can't remember anyone ever having lipstick, though. It would have been scrubbed off their mouths by Sister, anyway, saying they looked like Jezebels.

The older girls had a favourite pastime. They'd say that they were going 'catching'. I noticed them using mirrors or 'looking glasses' to throw reflections on the trees or garden walls and had a go myself a few times. I soon learned what 'catching' really was, though. It was 'catching' the sunlight and throwing or aiming the reflection towards the big boys' dorm. They were signalling their boyfriends! Don't ask me how anyone understood the signals. They were all lights and flashes to me and quite blinding. Maybe everyone knew Morse code or something. All I could see were arms waving from the boys' dorm windows. It was all fun and harmless, I guess. There was no way that they could rendezvous in the afternoons, with the padlocked doors and barred windows being the obstacles. Sometimes the boys used the mirror signals as well for the girls. Whenever one of the girls spotted the flashing lights, she'd run to the others and yell out, 'Hey, somebody's trying to "catch" us!' Then there'd be a mad rush to the windows, trying to make out the boy's figure or guessing who he might be.

The girls who had boyfriends wrote to them almost every day, even though some letters never got beyond the lines, but they kept them anyway. They must have had fun writing them, though. The boys' letters always got a good giggle out of them, for some of the letters were passed around the room for the other girls to read. Talk about laugh! I'd see them laugh and throw themselves on their beds, giggling and rolling around, holding their tummies tight, like they were about to split. Afterwards, the love letters would be taken back, folded neatly and stored in a biscuit tin or cardboard suitcases, only to be taken out again the next day, for another good laugh. They never seemed to tire of the same old ritual. I didn't have a clue what it was all about but I laughed along with them, anyway.

BOYS' DORMITORIES, BEAGLE BAY MISSION, 1958

About three o'clock, Sister would come and unlock the doors. The girls went to carry on with other work, or continue with their unfinished work, such as sewing or ironing. The kitchen girls went back to the dining hall to prepare the evening meal or supper and the colony kids would be sent home promptly. Usually, our own evening meals were being prepared at home as well, or the women would just sit outside on the lawns and talk before cooking their meals. Evening meals were prepared early for there was no electricity. People wanted to see what they were eating and there were only lamps or candlelight available. They had to be used sparingly for times were hard after the war.

After the meals, blankets or ground sheets were spread out and the young and old of the colony gathered to swap yarns. Family and friends joined each other and mothers settled their little ones. The people from the top-end of the Kimberley told their stories and whatever they could remember. Likewise, the Nyul Nyul mob, or locals, would share their tales. The locals had an advantage over the top-end people because they weren't hundreds of miles away from their traditional lands. They had their people around them and no one could erase the past from these old people and stop them telling their stories, despite the fact that their practices were forbidden. For as long as they were alive, there was hope of saving some things from their culture.

My mimis and other old girls told us about things that happened to them in their convent days. Some were sad some were funny but we listened with a yearning for more. Our appetites were insatiable. Someone would start off with… 'Remember that time Sister and Mary Anne…' and they'd all start talking at once.

We cried for more until our mums told us to go inside to sleep. We obeyed them silently but sadly.

THE NATIVE SISTERS

EVERY YEAR, MONTHS BEFORE CHRISTMAS, the Sisters ordered dress materials and the likes so that the women and girls could make their own clothes for their Christmas parcels. Children's clothes were also made and handed out before the Feast day. There'd be a mad flurry to get the clothes finished.

These girls were taught to sew and make all their clothing when they were considered old enough. They made frocks, children's clothing and even underwear, even though they were stiff cotton and unbleached. They made religious garments and just about everything else. Would-be brides and bridesmaids made their gowns and dresses, as well as their accessories. As soon as their intentions were made to the Sisters, the preparations began. The materials were not flash but were plain and simple, white, blue and pink cottons and laces. It was amazing how simple materials could be transformed into something so beautiful. So skilled were the Sisters and girls that the outfits were beautifully finished and the wedding party always looked gorgeous and handsome. They made such beautiful pictures in my mind, and I consider myself privileged to have witnessed these scenes when I

SEWING, BEAGLE BAY MISSION, 1950s

was small. I wish I could have taken photos of them to show the children of today just what had happened at church weddings so many years ago on the mission.

Come Christmas time, all the clothes were finished so that the women and children wore their new clothes at midnight Mass and again at morning Mass. I was now over three years old and Mum was back at the mission as the King family were going down south for their Christmas break. This was going to be my first midnight Mass at Beagle Bay that I could remember. I was so excited because no one ever took me to one before as far as I know. Their excuse was that I was still a baby and wouldn't understand about it and would fall asleep. Being woken up in the middle of the night, still feeling dopey but trying to hurry up, I dressed in silence, not knowing that my dress was back to front. Mum had the patience to re-dress me properly. I wanted so badly to see Baby Jesus being born in the stable in Bethlehem. Weeks prior to this, the nativity scene was brought out of storage and arranged in the church. I'd go there just about every day with the other children and kneel down in front of the scene and say baby prayers. I just couldn't wait for Christmas and Baby Jesus. Everybody had the Christmas spirit and the night time stories turned to the bible stories and the birth of Baby Jesus and how the Three Wise Kings followed the shiny star to find Him.

All during Mass I waited and waited for His appearance. I really didn't know what to expect but I did expect to see a flesh and blood baby. When we all arrived back home, I asked Mum why I didn't see Baby Jesus.

'You fell asleep and I didn't have the heart to wake you up,' she said. I felt so sad.

'Next time, wake me up, okay?' I asked her, not knowing that I had to wait another year for my next midnight Mass.

At around about the same time I started to notice some grown-up dark, young women in white and blue uniforms and wearing short veils. They looked so lovely in their clothing, so serene in their manner and movement. It must have been at Mass on a Sunday when I started to notice them. Everybody went to Mass on a Sunday so it must have been then. I would see the religious orders seated in their proper places but somehow failed to notice the others sitting behind them. I kept looking and looking at them until Mum pinched my arm and gave me the mouth sign. I always knew what messages the silent eyes and mouth signs held. When we got outside, I asked her about the ladies in white and blue. She told me that they were the Native Sisters and they wore different habits and were different to the other Sisters. They were our very own nuns. Those young women and girls felt that they had the calling and wanted to become like the white Sisters.

'How come they don't sit with the other Sisters?' I asked. 'How come my aunties don't dress like that?'

Silly me! I got the famous answer again. 'Wait! You'll know when you grow up. Okay?'

After that incident, I began to take more notice of those

NATIVE SISTERS WITH BISHOP RAIBLE, 1950s

young ladies in white and blue. They were our own native girls and most of them were my mum's cousins. They looked like the Sisters and yet they didn't look like them. I saw them in church or just walking around the convent gardens or helping with the work around the convent. They seemed to be following the white Sisters around or imitating their style of walking around in prayer with bowed heads. Those Native Sisters must have been there for a while, so how come I only just started to notice them?

Mum did eventually tell me that they lived in the novitiate away from the professed nuns and that was all she ever told me about them.

Only in June of 1996 did I learn a little more about the Order. I was privileged to speak to Aunty Vera Dann Kanagae and Aunty Biddy Kelly, two former Native Sisters and they spoke freely about those halcyon days of theirs. It's kind of funny about Aunty Vera because when she came to live in Broome after working at Balgo and Beagle Bay, she shared a big house with Mum and Aunty Susie Dolby for a few years. I never bothered to ask her then, perhaps it was irrelevant to me at that young age (ten or eleven, I think.)

I was told by the two ladies that Bishop Otto Raible wanted to know if any of the girls had a vocation to become a nun, to lead a religious life. There was a positive response from quite a few of the girls. They were not pressured into it; it was of their own will. So on 6 January 1940, six young girls began their vocational training at Beagle Bay. They were Katie Fraser, Lucy Dolby, Biddy Kelly, Vera Dann, Mary Albert and Teresa Dann. Monica Dolby was their cook and their Reverend Mother was Mother Augustine, an American, I believe. Later on, other young ladies from Lombadina mission joined them. Their order was called Regina Apostolata, Queen of the Apostles. The two old ladies said that they did not feel different from the white nuns in all the time they were there and they have only good memories of their short-lived convent life.

The order closed in 1947 because of the decline in vocation amongst other young girls. It was a sad day for the remaining nuns to witness the closure of their order and they found it very hard to accept but life goes on. Eventually some of the native Sisters left the mission or married; some chose to live their lives out on the mission. I am sure that most of those young ladies would have remained true to their vocation if it was at all possible.

I missed seeing those lovely ladies in white and blue whenever I'd go back to Beagle Bay for holidays. I wish I could put my hands back into the past and pull those sisters back to the present and show our young people of today how gentle and devoted they were to their calling, right to the last minute.

Everyone sang the hymns so beautifully at Mass and Benediction. The men with their deep voices and the women with their voices filling the church at sung Masses and Benediction at night. The religious sang too in their heavily accented voices, German and Irish. So did the young native ladies of religion. Beagle Bay had a very fine choir and musicians for the nuns taught most to read music and play the violin, piano and organ. Even when they came to Broome one could hear the difference in their singing and guess that they were Beagle Bay people. Mimi Alice was a fine singer herself and we knew it was so because she used to sing for us in the evenings and teach us to sing as well.

WILLY AND
ALICE

I DIDN'T SEE MY LULU WILLY AROUND THE MISSION.

He was away sick in Derby. I first saw him in 1949 when he was released from Bungarun after a term of fourteen years. I remember him as being a solidly built man with very fair skin and thick, light brown wavy hair. Fourteen years is a long time to be kept away from your family. He was certainly a handsome man like nearly all the other Kimberley men. He always wore khaki clothes and what we kids called a 'cowboy' hat. I hadn't seen him when I was on the mission and asked Mimi why Lulu wasn't at home anymore. She told me that before I was born and before Lulu got sick, he was doing God's work with Father Francis Huegel, picking up the sick people around the Kimberley to take them to Bungarun, so that the good Sisters could take care of them, because nobody else would. That was how mission people used to talk, always using the terms of God, the Blessed Virgin Mary, St Joseph or other saints' names in their conversations. They never used the name Jesus without blessing themselves with the sign of the cross or bowing their heads.

Many of the Sisters of St John of God were trained nurses and were much needed in the remote regions, especially in the early pioneering days of the Kimberley. Others were teachers but all were dedicated women who were committed to the missionary life. I may have been only about four years old plus but was old enough to know about the Sisters, Fathers and Brothers and of their good work. I kind of knew what Mimi and Mum told me about Lulu not being there; I just didn't know what Bungarun, the Kimberley and Derby were. I knew those places must have been far away, too far for me to have imagined. I didn't know what the Bungarun 'sick' or the leprosarium was either.

Before he got sick, Lulu and Father Francis drove all over the Kimberley, picking up those poor sick people from the stations, towns and camps. Lulu would come and go, come and go, hardly ever staying too long at home. All his daughters and Mimi Alice were very happy when he got back to the mission from his trips. At least they had him there for a few months at a time.

In 1935 they had a bad time coming to terms with Lulu having been sent to Bungarun. After all those years of picking up the sick people, my Lulu contracted the disease and he himself ended up in Bungarun. In time, I heard that he had the Bungarun sickness, the 'big sick' as it was called by the natives. One of the reasons I never visited him was that children were not allowed to visit anyone there and the other was being in the orphanage. I remember that Mimi, Mum and my aunties went to Bungarun from time to time to visit when some restrictions were lifted for visitors. What a great waste it was not having a grandfather around but I treasured the time I did have with him.

Whether he became a bitter man because of his illness and after doing all he could to bring the sick lepers for treatment, I really cannot say. He never said anything to me about that even when I got to adulthood; maybe it was because I never asked him, which was a bit unusual for me. Perhaps I was beginning to grow up. I wish I had asked him, though.

I'd like to think that he accepted his illness as God's will even though he may have been crying and dying inside, all alone, for the lost years without his wife and children and the loss of his childhood with mob. Maybe those were only some of the reasons he finally succumbed to the alcohol sickness. It was heartbreaking for Mimi, my aunties and for his grandchildren to see a once healthy and vibrant man become a broken-down man.

While Lulu was at Bungurun, Mimi had to find work to keep herself going otherwise she'd be up for vagrancy. Native people always carried 'silver' or coins, even sixpence pieces, in case they were pulled up by the police and charged with vagrancy. Mimi was employed by prominent citizens of Broome, Mr and Mrs Male, and later Mr and Mrs McDaniel, as a housekeeper but she was also 'loaned out' to other pearler's wives when the occasion arose. All these people belonged to the elite pearling fraternity of old Broome Town.

Back then, native women were more employable than the men, for good housekeepers, cleaners and washerwomen were hard to find. The white women of Broome just snapped these people up so quickly. The mission women were trained for such work and while they were cheap labour, the pearlers' wives enjoyed their own short-lived 'grand' life as society ladies in a small country town. They couldn't have had it better.

In 1949, shortly after my Lulu's release from Bungurun, both he and Mimi applied for a Certificate of Citizenship under the

MIMI ALICE'S CITIZENSHIP PAPERS

Natives (Citizenship Rights) Act 1944 Form 1. I have copies of their files and some of the requirements leave much to be desired. Here are some fine examples:

On Form 2 of the said Act is the Statutory Declaration which required natives to declare:

- *That they were natives under the Native Administration Act, 1905–1941 and over 21 years of age*
- *That they wish to become a Citizen of the State of Western Australia in accordance with the provisions of the Native (Citizenship Rights) Act 1944*
- *That for two years prior to the date hereof they have dissolved tribal and native association except with the respect to lineal descendants or native relations of the first degree.*

On the applications forms that had to processed by the Department of Native Affairs were questions such as:

- *Has the applicant ever served in the Armed Forces of the Commonwealth?*
- *Has the applicant dissolved tribal and native association for two years?*
- *Has the applicant adopted the manner and habits of civilised life?*
- *Where has he been domiciled within the last two years?*
- *Does applicant live according to white standards?*
- *Does applicant and his wife consort with natives?*
- *Does applicant and his wife visit the camps of native relatives, or do the relatives visit them?*

The list went on.

Thorough investigations, such as bank details and character references, on my grandparents were carried out and after the court hearing, they were granted native citizenship.

They had to go through the same rigmarole when they applied for their pension in 1960. An officer of the Department of Native Welfare (name changed in 1954) became their cheque warrantee. They were controlled and treated like children even when they were old and in poor health.

Lulu died on 15th June 1969, a couple of days before I had my baby, Dianne Barbara. Sadly, I never made it to his funeral because of that. Then Mimi followed him in October of that same year. I went to her funeral with some of my children. Even though age and illness were against her too, we all think she died of heartbreak and fretting for him.

In the end they must have been worth something to the Native Welfare for they were billed $94.00 each for their funerals.

By no means do I want to paint their marriage as being perfect but Mimi stuck with Lulu through thick and thin, sickness and health, ever since they married in the little mission church they helped build. That was the way of life for those people of our grandparents' time. None of them got divorced or even separated unless it was through death or the 'big sick'.

GROWING UP IN BROOME

HOLY CHILD
ORPHANAGE

I ENTERED HOLY CHILD ORPHANAGE on 2 May 1946, and left on 23 December 1948. Two years and seven months of my young life without my mum, in that lonely place. I was under both names: Betty Hussan and Betty Wright.

I'm a bit hazy about why I was taken to Holy Child but according to a letter from my mum to Mother Margaret, she advised her that she had been working in Derby since August 1945 and only went back to the mission for Christmas holidays. It was recorded that Mum made a private arrangement to have me placed at HCO for reasons I shall never know. I can only surmise that she could not have coped living in Beagle Bay as an evacuee with no financial support for nearly two years. To add to this, she must have been in limbo with the extradition order still in place. The Civil Defence Council was financially responsible for the evacuee children and the mission authorities were not.

So she took the opportunity to go to Derby to work and Mimi and my extended family took care of me. Perhaps certain pressure was placed on her by the Native Affairs and other authorities to send me to HCO for my best interests. They told her that if she came back to Broome, there would not be adequate accommodation available and she would probably go back to living in an undesirable locality: the Asiatic quarters, down the marsh, in Chinatown. If she did, then I would be taken off her. This certainly raises some doubt in my mind about the private arrangement. Some of this information was recorded in the Native Affairs files.

Even though this was a grey area when I was growing up, I have accepted the facts as I know them now, that times and set conditions were hard for every native man and woman. In all those years, I never asked my mum about it, mainly because I was brought up in a Western world and took for granted that we were a controlled people, that white people ruled us. Now it's too late. My mother and father are no longer here with me as they would have been the only ones who could have told me.

It would appear from the files that there was a personal vendetta against my mother and father because they were defiant and flaunted their relationship in front of the authorities, Native Affairs and the police.

I cannot recall my actual arrival at the orphanage, but I do remember being taken by a nun to a slim young girl waiting patiently outside the door. I was told that she was my Aunty Cissy and that she would take good care of me. I liked that Sister and my Aunty from that very first day. I learned that they shared the name of Cecilia, so when I got confirmed at the age of eleven in 1953, I also took the same name. Sister Cecilia taught Aunty and many of the girls to play the violin and I still think that Sister was the finest pianist and violinist I'd ever heard in my young life.

AUNTY CISSY AND MIMI ALICE

In later years, my cousin Sally, Aunty Barb's surviving twin and the one who was born a month after me, told me that she could remember very clearly about the day she arrived in Broome. I should mention here that all my childhood friends gave me a nickname many, many moons ago. It was, and still is, Grange. I can guarantee that they will still call me Grange when we'll be older and greyer and in our eighties, God willing.

'Truly, Grange, I remember the day the mission truck dropped us off in Chinatown. I remember that because Raymond Clement, Mummy's godson, was crying and crying for us because we were leaving the mission for good and I was still thinking about him and feeling sorry for him, when we arrived in Broome. When we got to Chinatown, I saw a little old Chinese lady stacking up cardboard boxes in front of her shop. There was a young Chinese girl, about ten years old, who was standing beside her. She had straight, long black hair almost to her waist, neatly plaited and tied with pink ribbons. What caught my eye was the beautiful cyclamen pink, silky top she wore. It was so beautiful, so simply gorgeous. I just stared and stared at this lovely little Chinese girl in the cyclamen pink top because I had never seen anything like it before. I found out later on that she was Mary Dep, daughter of the owners of Dep's Store. Then afterwards Uncle Benda came to pick us up and take us home.'

I knew that I had Aunties Cissy, Kudjie and Peggy living in Broome, so when I would eventually meet the other two it would be as a 'grown-up' child, not as a teeny-weenie baby. They had last seen me as a little baby at the mission. Both aunties had left the mission before I could really get to know them but I sure made up for lost time in Broome. Aunty Cissy kept telling me about them and that I'd be seeing my cousin Aggie Sesar for the first time ever, probably on the next visiting Sunday. In a way I felt a bit sad and nervous about meeting my cousins for it meant that I'd be sharing her with my grandparents now. In time, that feeling faded for I became very close to Aggie and then Charlie, when he was born later on. They were the children of my Aunty Kudjie and Uncle Jacob Sesar. Aunty also reminded me that I'd be seeing my own father who was still in close contact with Mum's family even though she was in Derby.

When I first saw Aunty Cissy I thought that she looked lovely. All my aunties were lovely looking women but here was an aunty, so young and so much closer to my age that I was a bit confused. She was of slim build, not very tall, with curly black hair tumbling down her shoulders and back. Her face was smooth and soft, a happy looking face. I liked her at once. Why wasn't this Aunty with her sisters in Beagle Bay? How come she'd had to go to the Broome orphanage and her sisters stayed on the mission? She was separated from them for years. I found out later in life, as usual, but that didn't stop me wondering during those years. You have to guess about the 'happenings'. You either find out by accident or when life is almost over for everyone, or after people have finally passed onto another life.

Those days and nights at the orphanage were lonely for me at first. I didn't have my little mates from the mission with me. Now there were strange faces. All of us girls had no mothers here with us. Some of us had sisters, aunties and even cousins but they weren't our mothers. No one could take the place of mothers, no matter how 'bad' our mothers were made out to be. I just couldn't feel the love and warmth of my family in there. It wasn't fun anymore. It wasn't home anymore. I wanted my mum.

The dorm was different to the ones at the mission. Here, the little girls slept at one end of the dorm while the bigger girls slept at the top end. It was one huge room with rows and rows of beds, army style. I had to sleep in my own bed just like the others and I cried almost every night from sheer loneliness. I didn't have my Aunties Giggy, Bella or Binyu anymore, only Aunty Cissy but she was just a child herself. She had to sleep in the big girls' section, away from me. When Aunty found out about all the crying, she'd sneak over and get me, letting me sleep at the leg end of her bed. Before the bell rang in the morning, she'd take me back to my bed so that the others wouldn't snitch on us. Anyway, she didn't care if she got into trouble. Let them belt me, she'd say. She just didn't want to see me cry. Thank God for Aunty Cissy being in the orphanage with me. She was another of my mothers. She was my eighth and littlest mother.

Aunty had some good friends her own age but she took me everywhere with her and her friends, even while doing her own chores. She and her best friend Pena Ozies were inseparable and I tagged along with them most of the time. Pena didn't mind, after all she was my Aunty's best friend. When they left the orphanage, both girls found work at the hospital and after a while they left Broome, going in different directions: Pena to Katherine, Northern Territory, I think and Aunty to Port Hedland after she married Uncle Tommy Clarke, brother to Uncle Gerry. Aunty had never forgotten her friend Pena because she still spoke about her during all those years apart from each other. Even her children knew about their friendship.

At HCO there was an older woman. She was in charge of all the girls, a kind of house mother to us. Everyone called her Aunty Bella and I wondered whether my own Aunty Bella was named after her, because I found out that she was a niece of my Lulu Willy and also the sister of Aunty Barb. Some of the girls said that she always favoured her relatives, such as Aunty Cissy and the Howard girls, Lucy and Cissy. Whether she did or not is not for me to say, after all I'm also of one blood with her. Still and all, she took no nonsense from the girls, big ones and little ones. She was one strict lady and kept everyone on their toes but she was a loving person and was loved by many of the orphanage girls. Perhaps because she was taken away from her mother and family when she was about seven years old and knew what it was like to never see your mother again. There had to be a hidden, meaningful reason behind her mothering nature.

Every Saturday she saw that the girls sorted out their Sunday best for Mass. We all had to have our frocks, undies, socks, sandals or shoes ready. No mucking around last minute or there'd be a price to pay. No one wanted to be in trouble, that's for sure. All the same, she gained a lot of love and respect from those same little girls when they grew up. They're the ones who still watched out for her when she became older and frailer, even if only to keep her company for a few hours a day. We have to remember that she was the nearest person to being a mother for the orphaned or displaced girls.

On Sundays, we lined up at the front gate in readiness for the walk to the church. It was quite a distance to the church and we had to walk in pairs, starting off with the little ones in front and the bigger ones taking up the rear, followed by the Sisters. Walking to Mass was okay for me but I was always so weary on the long walk back. I'd say to my Aunty, 'I can't walk anymore,

Aunty. My legs feel slack.' Then she'd pick me up and piggyback me to the home.

When we got back to the orphanage, parents or relatives would be waiting to take their children out for the day. The first Sunday for me found Mimi Alice waiting for us and I was so happy to see her. She told me that Mum couldn't pick me up because she was working in Derby but my dad would be there. On the walk to Chinatown, where my family lived, I was so excited that I didn't notice how long the walk took. It must have been over two miles but I didn't care. My legs no longer felt slack.

It was good to see my dad again. I had seen him in Beagle Bay when he visited Mum a few times over the years. Even though I cannot recall him very well, I do remember him as my flesh and blood dad who gave me piggyback rides to the shops and around Chinatown and called me his *Mymuna*, according to my Mimi.

Still working for Streeter & Male, Dad left for Darwin in 1949 (just after I left HCO). I remember the day he left. My Aunty Bella and Aunty Binyu picked me up and ran outside when they heard a plane overhead, heading north into the blue sky.

'That's your daddy in that plane. He's going to Darwin but you can go and visit him.'

I never saw him again and over the years my parents went their separate ways. Dad did return to Broome in the 1960s with his new family. (At some point my father had returned to Malaysia and married.) He had wanted to see me but I was living in Port Hedland with my own growing family. He was going to retire and live in Malacca as he was now a sick man who wanted to go back home. I had it in my mind that he never bothered about me, so why should I go? I think what influenced my thinking was that a couple of older Malay men used to tell me, even at the ripe old age of five, that Eusop never wanted me and that's why he went to Darwin. I never forgot those words.

When Dad left Broome and I got a bit older, I mentally built a cocoon-like shell around me, like a steel mesh. I never allowed myself to think about him because in my childish mind, I thought that he didn't want me any more and that was why he never contacted me.

Years later, after I read the files, I realised how how wrong I was. I became very emotional and silently wept for months without telling any of my family. I had never confided in anyone about my hidden agony and because of this found it difficult to express or explain this heartrending anguish to them.

Anyway, I did find out that my dad loved me and never denied his parentage of me. It was circumstances and the authorities who controlled native people that parted families in the first place. I discovered that he used to send me food parcels and clothes to the mission and later on at HCO. I was given those things but always thought Mum had sent them. The Sisters never told me who sent them when handing me the parcels. I took it for granted that they were from Mum.

When I think of my father now, I wish I could have met up again with him. Of all the mistakes or decisions I have made, this was one of the biggest mistakes ever and I'll regret it for the rest of my days. Now both my parents are gone and I will never find out anything more. I have accepted this now, but I am afraid I will never find closure for my spiritual healing.

❖

On my first visit to Aunty Kudjie's and Uncle Jacob's everyone hugged and kissed me, saying that I looked the spitting image of Aunty Cissy. I didn't really believe them because Aunty was too pretty for me. When I grew older I'd tell her that if she was white, she'd look just like Ann Blyth, the film star. When my girlfriends at school played 'bagsing the film stars' they all bagsed to be Cissy Wright because they said she looked as pretty as a film star and they all wanted to be film stars themselves. They simply ignored the more famous Hollywood stars like Rita Hayward and Betty Grable. That's kids for you.

I noticed a little chubby girl sitting on the floor, and that was the first time I laid eyes on Aggie, my cousin. Aggie was their only child at that time, a couple of years younger than me. Later on Aggie and I started to play together, until it was time to go back to the orphanage. Like all good things, the day did not last long enough. I didn't want to go back with Aunty and I kicked up a big stink. Mimi and Dad didn't want me to go either. She promised that she'd take me out of HCO as soon as my mum came home. I must have been satisfied with that for I returned to the orphanage.

Aunty kept telling me that it was the government ways that made life difficult for the native people and there wasn't much we could do about it. That's why the missions and orphanages were established. I do know that I left the orphanage before Aunty did but it wasn't that long a time. Despite all that I still wanted to know how come I had to go back when Aggie could stay at home with Aunty and Uncle. It wasn't fair.

On one occasion, I went to visit the mob down the marsh when Uncle Jacob showed us a revolver that he was cleaning. Actually, Aggie and I went into their bedroom to play with dolls and make-up and didn't notice Uncle with the gun until he pointed it up to the ceiling. He warned us not to even think of touching the gun otherwise 'you know what'. It was a good-looking black gun, something like a German Luger, not like a cowboy's six gun. So he locked it away in the wardrobe and we forgot all about it.

It must have been a few months later that Aggie and I thought about the gun. No one was around so we decided to look at it again while we had the chance. Aggie knew where the key was kept and opened the door while I grabbed a chair to climb up. I saw it and quickly grabbed it, holding it with one hand. Next thing I knew, my little skinny hand was pulled down to the floor with the sheer weight. As I was falling down, I had tried to use my other hand to steady the weight but no good; it happened too fast. The gun hit the floor first and then my head landed on it. I almost passed out. I only felt a big lump on my throbbing head. Aggie rushed to my aid but couldn't do much for me. What did we know about first aid, anyway?

Uncle didn't tell us that the gun was too heavy for us to hold and we never thought about it. It looked so easy in the movies for the men to hold a six gun, twirl it around and smoothly holster it. Of course we somehow managed to put it back and locked the wardrobe door. We never told anyone about it and never dared to even think about touching it again. Luckily it wasn't loaded.

Being in the orphanage meant that I had to go to kindergarten school as well, for I was now of kindergarten age. We had to walk there, which was almost the same distance as the church, as both were on the same block of land. I liked going to school, learning the songs, nursery rhymes and fairy tales, going to catechism lessons with Mother Margaret, the most lovable Irish nun ever. She was very old but in spite of her age, she certainly wasn't senile. All of us kids just loved to hear her talk in her rich, broad Irish brogue, telling us stories about her Emerald Isle, teaching us to sing Irish lullabies. How she must have missed Ireland, coming out to this strange land when she was a teenager, she was only a child herself. She never let me forget that she was my Mimi Alice's godmother and that Mimi was one of the first native children she saw at the landing, when they disembarked from the ketch. So I had to mind myself in front of her almost all of the time.

She took us for catechism lessons under the big mango tree at the convent. I learned a great deal about God and Jesus, the Virgin Mary, St Joseph and just about all the angels and saints, not forgetting the Patron Saint of Ireland, St Patrick himself, who drove out all the snakes from Ireland. Oh no! Mother Margaret never let a day go by without praising St Patrick. There was a holiday on that day every year and we were reminded to wear the colour of green at Mass and all day long if possible. Life was a breeze being a kindy kid with Mother Margaret in charge.

After kindergarten, we had to change into our dungaree dresses or pinafores and do chores, whether it was feeding the chooks, collecting eggs or helping in the kitchen and dining room. I didn't have to do work at the mission but I soon learned about it here. Again emphasis was placed on time management. Everything had to be done properly and finished on time otherwise we'd be boxed around the ears, which usually had a good effect on the more defiant girls. It may have stung for a while but so what. We laughed away our tears and woes. After work was done, there was time to play at the back of HCO, in a partly cleared playground.

The most popular games were rounders, hopscotch and fly which were really enjoyed by us all. Fly was a game something like triple jump but played with a number of sticks lying about a foot apart, in a straight line, with the first one placed about a yard away from the rest. It was the anchor and could not be moved at all. We had to run up to the sticks, stepping between them, careful not to displace any and then jump over the last one. The jump was measured and the last stick moved to that mark. The sticks in the middle could then be moved and placed at various lengths between the first stick and the last one, which could only be moved by the last jumper. She had to make the jump difficult for the others by staggering the length of the sticks like placing three sticks about a foot apart, then the next two about a yard apart and the rest of them about a foot apart again. As the distance between the sticks got longer, the girls made their long run like a cricket bowler and just flew between the sticks to make their jump, thus the name 'fly'. If no one could beat the last winning jump, the game was over. You can bet your last two bob that the winner was always challenged the next day.

So things weren't too bad for me in the long run. It was the loneliness and the separation from my family in Chinatown and Beagle Bay that were the worst things imaginable.

I will never forget my first Christmas at Holy Child, though. Not the actual day but the day the presents were distributed to us at the orphanage. There are many 'I'll never forget' stories in this book but this was the strongest of all my childhood memories. I think that some of the presents were donated by the local business people, as well as the usual charitable organisations through the church. Regardless of where we came from, we all received a present, some lollies and cordial drinks.

All the little girls' names were called out and they received their presents and sat down again, opening their boxes and packages. They sounded happy and showed each other their teddy bears or pretty dolls. Finally, I heard my name being called out and jumped up to receive mine. I couldn't contain myself any longer and started to tear open the package, expecting to see a pretty doll, for it had the same sort of wrapping paper and the same size package as the other girls.

Well! I stopped dead in my tracks and burst out crying. What I saw was a doll all right! It was a black doll, not even a pretty one. It was the ugliest black doll with the woolliest, fuzzy-wuzzy hair. It was a kind of rubbery, plastic gollywog type of doll. I had seen gollywogs before but nothing as ugly as that one. It would have been an insult to the gollywog kingdom. Tears were running down my cheeks. I was devastated. I couldn't hide my disappointment; it was so evident from my tears.

I am sure that it was a reject from the factory. People couldn't possibly make such ugly dolls for children, could they, especially for four year olds? To make things worse, I was the only one out of all the little girls who had an ugly black doll. Aunty Cissy didn't have to ask what all the tears were about. She grabbed me by the hand and went bouncing up to the front to see if she could exchange it for another, telling Sister about it and showing it to her but there were no other presents left. So I was stuck with it.

I hated that doll, not because it was black, not because it was a gollywog type but because of its ugliness. I tried to throw it away, hoping someone would put it in the rubbish bin, but no, it always came back to me, because the whole orphanage knew it belonged to me. The other girls always laughed and made fun of me for having that doll. I'd sling it across the room hoping it would break but no go! I even tried to leave it at Aunty Kudjie's but they made sure I always took it back. Don't forget your Christmas present, they'd remind me. As if I'd ever forget it! I even tried to swap it for one of the pretty dolls but no such luck. It was a truly terrifying looking doll.

I brought that doll home with me when I left the orphanage but I can't remember where it got to after that. It must have been so ugly that nobody wanted to even touch it, so it could easily have been thrown in the rubbish heap and burned or something like that. After that one doll, I was never given a doll for Christmas or birthdays, even though I always yearned for one. I somehow wish I did have that the ugly doll here so that I could show my children and all my grandchildren how terribly cruel it was for me that Christmas of 1946.

I can't really complain about the orphanage in the short time that I was there but I suppose others may see it differently. Even when I left the orphanage I was still under the protective and pastoral care of the St John of God Sisters at St Mary's Primary School. (It was only when I checked the records in recent years that I found out I was officially regarded as a 'ward of the state'.)

Sure, we had our share of the hard and sad times during our growing-up years but most of my memories are of the good times I shared with my friends and of the foolish things we did from time to time. Whenever we were punished for the mischief we caused, we knew that we only had ourselves to blame. Perhaps we only thought of the fun we could have, like playing tricks and jokes on others and not really being thoughtful of their feelings.

I think that the saddest thing about being in the orphanage was that the girls never went home, as far as I could remember,

AN ORPHANAGE OUTING — MYSELF, SHIRLEY THOMPSON,
PATSY DOWNS, MARJORIE ANGELA, SALLY DEMIN c1948

for holidays at Christmas time. Some of my best friends were there from baby time until they turned sixteen or thereabouts and we all parted company, a lot of them going back to their country to find their families. They did go to the beachside for camping though, for the Sisters had a beach house at Reddell Beach and a small truck for their transport.

The Sisters ran the place to the best of their ability and knowledge, and the girls' welfare and education was always taken care of. In Broome, when we catch up with each other and yarn about the old days, most of us would say that we would prefer being brought up by the nuns than being placed in other institutions, not that we knew first hand about them but only from what we heard from other people and reading about them. If it weren't for the nuns, priests and brothers in the Kimberley we probably never would have had a chance to be educated or eventually have higher education for our children of today.

The majority of people who were brought up by the missionaries in the Kimberley will only have good and positive things to say, despite the hardship they suffered and endured in those lean years and trying conditions. They were courageous, dedicated and committed men and women who helped our people in more ways than one. My mimis and lulus and other mission people never spoke ill of the religious orders who were family to them. Their lives continued with their ceaseless work for the church and the disadvantaged people in the towns and communities. They visited the sick and healthy, the old and new, the rich and the poor of the parish, in their homes or in the hospitals, almost every week, walking from home to home, just checking in on their physical and spiritual health.

There have been stories published by Aboriginal people who were in other homes or missions and whose lives have been left fragmented by their experiences. One reads, with horror, of their beatings, their floggings and their severe punishment. News travelled like wildfire in a small community and whenever anyone got a flogging for something or other, the whole mission knew about it. I have been told of such by my own people but have not seen anything myself. When I was smaller, I could not imagine any grown-up person being flogged. I can only write about the couple of swift cuts on our hands from the cane or our ears being boxed when we were punished at school for misbehaving.

On 23rd December 1948, Mum took me out of the orphanage for holidays to Beagle Bay and later advised the HCO that she would be keeping me. We went back to Broome so that I could begin proper school, going into the first class at St Mary's. My kindy friends were all there as well, all of us being a bit shy and frightened at seeing so many other kids, big and small. Some of them cried and cried nearly all day, calling out for their mums and dads. Others settled in well because they had family there.

Nearly all of us were barefoot but we were used to it. Of course there were some who had nice shoes or sandals or even white sandshoes to wear. Most of the girls wore pretty cotton frocks while the orphanage girls had to wear plain, ugly blue cotton ones, with white bias binding sewn onto the front, making a false collar. These were the Holy Child school uniform and by that outfit, everyone in town knew who lived at the orphanage. No wonder, years later in the fifties, the girls were nicknamed the Blue Army, when seen walking in double file from the orphanage to the school.

This reminds me of the times when the health nurses visited school to check us out for head lice, scabies and general health. Even if one didn't have head lice, some of us still had our hair sprinkled with DDT powder and wound around with calico. I'm sure they used recycled nappies from the maternity ward. We were made to sit on the school verandah having passersby look at us. We sure felt like monkeys after delousing themselves.

There was a time in the 1950s when there was an outbreak of diphtheria around the place and we all had to be vaccinated in the leg. It wasn't too bad but the next day everyone at school was limping. It was painful but watching everyone limping around made it look so funny, especially when we spotted the Blue Army rounding the bend, marching on one bended knee each, bopping up and down in rhythm.

When I was in little school, as it was called, we began to learn the ABCs and the 123s. It was hard at first, trying to sound the letters and then to write them down but it got easier in time. The same went for the numbers. It took practice to do things properly. We didn't use pencils and paper at little school; we had to use chalk and black slates to write and draw, scratching laboriously, using dusters or rags to wipe the slates clean for the next lesson or next day.

Every day at little school, we'd watch out for the ice-cream man every playtime. He'd start ringing his bell from a long distance, letting us know that he was heading our way. He rode a bike attached to a sort of mini ice-cream van. As soon as he stopped by the roadside, kids from every direction ran over to him, waving their one shilling and two-bob pieces, singing out, 'Me, Mr Torres' or 'Me, Uncle Joe,' all vying for his attention. He attracted old people as well as young mothers with babies who lived in nearby houses. All over town he sold his ice-creams; they were absolutely the finest ever made anywhere. Uncle Joe was also a talented musician who played music to anyone who listened. Even when he lived next door to the Sesars down the marsh, he played his ukulele and we thought he was solid. I believed he had his own small band years ago in the romantic Broome of the pearling era.

All the kids liked Mr Torres, the ice-cream man. He had family in Broome but one day we heard that he went to Darwin and we all felt so sad. It wasn't the same buying ice-cream in the shops. We sure missed Uncle Joe when he left Broome.

DOWN-THE-MARSH KIDS

AUNTY CISSY FINALLY CAME OUT of the orphanage in 1949 when she was sixteen. I had been out for about a year because Mum was now working at the Broome District Hospital as a domestic, sometimes as a cook, wardsmaid or as a kitchen hand. She had outlived her punishment a long time ago (sentence not specified) and at last she had found 'adequate employment' in Broome. She was living down the marsh at Aunty Kudjie's but still had to prove that she had found 'adequate accommodation' with her sister and brother-in-law, so for the time being we lived at Aunty's. Of course, Mum and my grandparents did eventually move from Aunty's to another house, just at the back of the Sun Pictures, not too far away and still on the marsh, just a couple of minutes walk away.

All in all, family life in Chinatown for my cousins and me was spent between the two houses and all the other haunts around the place. Our parents made sure that we went to school but we did have the occasional wag. We were always caught out in the end, no matter how much we tried to cover up the waggings.

Uncle Jacob Sesar held the family together in Broome as he was married to Aunty and was beholden to my grandparents and their daughters who had left the mission to live in Broome and Port Hedland. The other daughters would gradually leave the mission to make their own destiny, finding their future husbands and having their own children. On leaving the confines of the convent life, they in turn all ended up at Uncle's and Aunty's place, down the marsh. My Lulu Willy spent a lot of years in Bungarun, so they took us all in, Mimi Alice as well, even though the two in-laws avoided each other, which was the custom. It looked so funny when Mimi ran into the room to hide herself, not coming out until Uncle had left. Sometimes she'd be cooped up in the room for hours. Uncle and Mimi were traditional people and respected their cultural law so that was the way it had to be. It was like mortal sin to them if they broke the law.

We were told to let Mimi know whenever the sons-in-laws or even the prospective ones, came around to visit, not fully understanding the significance of the custom of avoidance. Mimi told us that those men were our mothers' 'straight' or intended husbands but most of her daughters were spoken for, anyway. I often asked her how come the men were so old for my aunties. She'd only give me the same looks that Mum always did.

Even when the sisters moved out after they married, the house down the marsh was the centre of everyday life for all of them. Everyone would pull up there, have a chat or something to eat, then go shopping or do other business. Aunty would usually have fish and rice for lunch, for Uncle always went fishing down the creek, most times never coming back empty handed. Afternoon time, other people joined up and soon a blanket would be spread on the ground outside and they'd start playing poker.

If we weren't hanging around the adults, we either played down the dry marsh flats kicking football or playing chasey with other Chinatown kids or played card games ourselves, not for money, only matchsticks though, because we had no money. Playing for money came later on when we saw other kids playing for real. Sometimes we watched the young Malay boys play soccer. We thought they looked really stupid bumping their heads with the ball and not picking it up with their hands. Quite obviously, we were ignorant of the game.

Bikes to native kids were as scarce as hen's teeth back in those days. Only the lucky ones or rich kids owned bikes. Some of them let us ride them from time to time. Anyone who had lots of material possessions, which we certainly lacked, was called a rich kid. They didn't have to have millions of pounds lying around the joint. To us they were rich, shop shut. We had to 'friend them up' for a go on their bikes.

Chinatown kids and down-the-marsh kids made do with any sort of resources around them to build bikes or carts, even going to the rubbish dump to scavenge around for parts and old bike frames, wheels and handlebars. It didn't matter that they had to walk a five-or-six-mile round trip, carrying the parts on their shoulders all the way back home. It didn't matter if the re-constructed bike had a small front wheel and a bigger rear wheel, which looked utterly ridiculous, as long as it could go.

Have you ever seen six or seven kids on one bike, all at the same time? You'd probably say 'can't be' or 'never'. Well, kids in Broome in the forties and fifties did just that. I wouldn't be at all surprised if it still goes on. If one of our friends had a bike, especially a big man's bike, we'd all jump on it with the strongest boy as the rider, an extra kid on the saddle behind him, one on the handlebar, two on the straight bar and one on the carrier above the back wheel. If the kids were smaller, there was room for seven kids. We just squeezed in any old how. Goodness knows how we never had an accident. We'd cruise all the way to wherever and all the way back, screaming and yelling or just singing our heads off with any old tune.

Sometimes there'd be about ten kids running behind, holding the seat and begging to have a go. Or kids riding tyreless bikes around town or down the marsh, not caring that they'd be having a bumpy ride or that the wheel could buckle under them.

Besides playing down the marsh for shillings and pence, we found time to play with toys, old dolls, cars, popguns and such.

PLAYING ON SHORT STREET WITH COUSINS AND FRIENDS—
BILLY WRIGHT, CHARLIE SESAR (DEC.), JOY SMITH, RICHARD CHARLES (DEC.),
GILBERT SESAR, BONNIE SESAR, AGGIE SAMPIE

Sunshine Milk tins were punctured through the top lid and bottom, wire threaded through them then filled with sand and pulled behind us. Old tyres were pushed along by a couple of kids, while some kids bent themselves into other tyres, asking someone to push them along until they got dizzy, while others tried to ride bikes for the first time. The boys also made wagon carts from old wooden fruit boxes, old pram wheels and some rope to pull them along. They never got tired of making use of discarded things that people no longer wanted anymore.

Sometimes we got to get out of town, and our mob of kids would wait for old man Jumbood to pack up his horse and cart with stores for Brother Bob Lawrence out at Coconut Well. We'd all hop on board and thoroughly enjoy the long ride there. We helped him in the garden and played in the bush and made up our own games. Then he'd take us home the same way.

A lot of times, Uncle Tommy and Aunty Peggy would take us to the butcher paddock and we'd have a good time trying to ride the mules that my Uncle Subu Samut and Tommy Dean rode around the place.

Uncle Jacob worked for Streeter & Male down at their boat yard, right down back of their big general store, near the foreshore and creek, building luggers and dinghies for the pearling mob. Besides building boats, he built houses and dinghies for them too. He built houses for the other people after his normal working hours, during weekends and holidays or during lay-up season.

Life was like that in Broome, just going along at your own pace, knowing that things would be finished sooner or later, no matter how long it took. Uncle Jacob was a bush carpenter just like Lulu Willy and a very good one too. He had a good name for his work within the Chinatown community, to build and do repair and maintenance work for the shopkeepers and neighbours. He was also the best fisherman and hunter in the world, to all of us kids anyway.

When I had first set eyes on Aunty and Uncle, I noticed that he was much older that she was. I noticed too, that my other aunties had married their men who were as young as themselves or only a few years older. Years ago, Mimi Alice told me that Aunty fell in love with Uncle when she first laid eyes on him. She was still a sweet, young teenager and, right or wrong, she said she was going to marry Jacob Sesar one day.

'I'm gonna marry that Jacob Sesar. You wait and see,' she said with determination.

Of course no one took any notice of her. It was only a young girl dreaming. My grandparents had no problems with that notion. It was the trauma of getting permission from the church and the Native Affairs people that made them sick, more so the Native Welfare. Back and forth, back and forth the letters went, with the length of time between mail dispatches making the waiting worse for words. There were no trunk calls between Broome and Perth those days, let alone between Broome and Beagle Bay! It wasn't until 1967 that people could make operator connected trunk calls and in 1975 when STD became available. That was how our people had to live under the government system. They had no right to their own lives; they were nobody. Finally permission came through and they married in 1944. They remained together for the rest of their lives, having raised ten children.

Where we lived were four houses all in a row. All four were built on concrete stilts, being on lower ground than the other houses, the reason being that the high tides would flood the marsh basin and overflow onto the streets, shops and other dwellings. Some houses had the seawater coming right through their wooden floors. We also fished from the windows catching whiting and bream while others tried their hand at throwing their nets in the shallows for mullet. Best of all, we dived from the windows and swam from the steps into the swirling waters, having the time of our lives, yelling and screaming, ducking and diving, holding our breath and swimming under water until we tired ourselves.

The Sun Pictures in Chinatown also went under water and on picture nights, with the water seeping through the cracks in the lower walls and wire fence, we had to move onto the higher level or put up with wet feet. After the show, people waded out onto the streets to higher ground, husbands and boyfriends carrying their ladyloves, little kids crying and grizzly because they didn't want to step into the cold water.

The Roe kids (old Eddie Roe's family) were lucky because their dad or big brothers waited for them with a dinghy to ferry them home. They lived further down from us and had more water to cross. Not like us, poor things. We had to wade back home in the dark, trying to keep the little sleepy kids awake, because they were too heavy for us to carry piggyback. Bigger kids would sometimes frighten us by yelling, 'Yor-yor! Look out shark coming for you guys!' In our haste we'd slip and slide, getting our clothes wet: shivering until we reached the steps to safety. No worries. We'd do the same thing come next high tide.

Another old place we played at was at Mimi Dora Smith's house. Sometimes we'd sleep over because it was a family gathering place and there were plenty of kids there. That was the best place for telling ghost stories, because it looked scary at night and there were some good yarn spinners amongst the grown-ups. No one can beat old people for telling them. Some of the kids who lived there were Joy Smith, Mimi's daughter, and Pinker Albert, a cousin and a good mate of ours from childhood days.

So you can imagine how many kids went to school from down the marsh and from the up the hill area. There were quite a lot. We all met up near the old railway tracks off Carnarvon Street and wended our way to both schools. When it was neap tide, most of us cut across the marsh to get to school. During my school years at St Mary's there were no canteen or tuckshop facilities available. Kids from all directions had to walk to school in the morning and go back home for lunch. All in all, we kids from Chinatown area had to walk nearly four miles a day, to and from school, twice a day, if we didn't bring our lunches. It wasn't too bad because there were dozens of kids doing the same thing, walking to and fro. We talked most of the way and that seemed to make the distance less that it really was. We didn't worry about it, the distance, I mean. Anyway, we had no choice in the matter.

It was the hot weather and walking in the heat that was the real problem. As some of us had no sandals or shoes to wear, our feet burned in the hot sand. When we did have footwear, we either lost them or they had worn out and it took a while to get replaced, depending on finance. We'd jump from grass patch to grass patch or stand under the trees for a few minutes for our feet to cool off, then run full speed to another tree. Quite often we shared our sandals and shoes, one kid wearing a left side and the other a right side, even if they didn't quite fit properly, size wise. The big boys often carried the little kids on their backs or shoulders until they found a shady spot to put them down.

Sometimes we'd make sacrifices for the poor souls in purgatory and walk barefoot in the hot sand. We'd say that our sacrifices lessened the hours for someone's soul to get into heaven. It made us feel good in spirit but not our poor little burned feet. We still kept making sacrifices, though.

If it was big tide, it was another story. As soon as someone spotted the gleaming sea water of the incoming tide, he'd yell out, 'Big tide, big tide. Come on you guys.' We'd repeat the cries to the kids behind us and start running full speed ahead and *jubul* into the water, head first, clothes and all, shoes and all (whoever had any). Gone were the sacrifices and good intentions; they flew out of our little heads and minds and were gone with the wind.

It felt so cool and refreshing after walking in the heat. We'd splash around and swim to the other side, nearest to the shopping area and wade our way to our house.

When our mums saw us in our now almost dry clothes they'd tell us to hurry up and eat so that we could get back to school in time for the afternoon lessons. They'd be mad at us for swimming in the sea with our school clothes and told us to go back to school with the same salty clothes because that was our punishment.

'Let them smell you guys. You guys want to smell like salt and fish. More you want to go swimming.'

That was just a normal day for us when it was big tide season, just swimming around then going back in our salty clothes. It was the other days that got us in deeper trouble, when we swam and followed the tide beyond the mangroves edge and walked through the swamp, spearing small fish, sea snakes, especially the small stripey ones, the bugul bugul and then looking for the small crabs for bait. We followed the tide right down to Morgan Creek and played there until *goomboon* time. Only the fear of the goomboons made us move fast out of the darkening mangroves. Otherwise, we didn't have a care in the world about going home.

Just about all the down-the-marsh kids played in the mangroves after the tide receded. Cassy Torres, who lived in the house next door to Uncle Jacob's, was older than us and we considered him our leader and hero. Besides our gang, there was also Lenny and Tony Sampi, and Pinker who were about our age and considered as 'big boys' to us.

It was Cassy and Lenny who taught us how to spear the sea snakes and mullet and make small fish traps to catch smaller fish. They taught our boy cousins how to make the spears and sinkers with scrap lead and wires that they scavenged around Chinatown and the rubbish tip. They showed us their secret hideaways in the mangroves and we imagined ourselves as mangrove fairies, elves and leprechauns, or jungle warriors. Even when the marsh was dried up during the low tides we managed to play there and sometimes ended up near the One Mile camp looking for tailor fruit or backtracking to the bomb holes.

When we emerged from the mangroves, it was a wonder that we weren't mistaken for goomboons ourselves. We must have looked quite a sight, with mud splattered on us from head to toe, on our clothes and up to our knees. From a distance, we'd spot our mums or dads stripping the leaves off the mangrove branches, getting ready for us. We'd start whimpering as we neared them, the whimpering turning into loud cries before we even got smacked. As usual we never tried to run away and got a couple of good whacks on our skinny legs, as we ran around in circles. I tell my kids now that we must have been little rascals for not considering the time and money our parents had to find to buy our clothes.

Next day, Sister Ignatius would ask us of our whereabouts the day before. We'd say nothing but if she persisted we'd end up telling her. Our mums never wrote notes to the Sisters to make up excuses for us. They told us that we had to tell the tale ourselves, whether we lied about it or told the truth was up to us because they sure wouldn't lie for us. We told the Sisters the truth when asked because if they had to visit our mums, the truth would come out anyway. So we didn't risk the double dose of punishment. It was a neverending saga, these adventures of ours.

One of the highlights of the year were the sideshows. The sideshows drew people into Broome from all over the place, especially from the stations. The others were the Slim Dusty and Buddy Williams Shows. They drew packed houses. One year in particular we were privileged to see the Redex Trial drivers stop over in Broome. All the kids scratched their names and addresses on the cars. Months later Aggie received a letter from one of the drivers. We thought it was great but she never wrote back.

Every year we celebrated Guy Fawkes Day with a bonfire in town and everyone brought their crackers, skyrockets and other fireworks to set off. We didn't know who Guy Fawkes was then, but we still celebrated the day. Of course we found out who he was in history class later on. I sure felt sorry for Guy Fawkes; he was just following his conscience.

We would save up to buy fireworks for weeks before the 5th of November. One year though, my cousin Charlie forgot he had left some in his trouser pocket and somehow a spark must have got into the pocket and set off the crackers. There was explosion, smoke and fire coming from the trousers and someone rolled him over to put out the flames. He was taken to hospital and thank God he wasn't severely burnt. All the cousins cried for Charlie that night.

Some things always seemed to happen to Charlie. One time ago, he was trapped in a water pipe near the state school where the new bore water plant was located. Aggie, Tracey and a few of us decided to have a look at the water gushing from the pipes. I don't know how Charlie got down the pipe and thank God it didn't have water in it. Anyway, after all of us were crying and screaming, people came running from their houses to see what was wrong. I think the police and Public Works people came to the rescue. Of course, we all got told off and sent home and we copped it again at home.

ALL KINDS OF GAMBLING

LIVING DOWN THE MARSH SURE WAS GREAT. Within walking distance were the shops, the Sun Pictures, the Roebuck Hotel, the swimming areas, the gambling houses and a few Chinese restaurants. If it wasn't for the gambling houses, nearly every one of us (natives) would go hungry, with hardly any food in the house or any good clothes to wear, only raggedy ones.

There were two gambling houses run by two Chinese men, Mr Dep and Baldhead Tailor. Baldhead Tailor's place was around the back of Ah Kim's. He ran chiffa as well as card games, the same as Mr Dep. Chiffa was a kind of Chinese lottery that nearly everyone played. If they didn't know much about it at first, they soon knew how to play it later on. It was drawn twice a day, the first draw at noon and the second one in the evening. It usually paid healthy dividends with better divvies during the lay up: more bets laid meant more money in the pool. Even kids had a bet with their one shilling and two shillings, trying to win picture money. On good betting days, the divvy might pay up to two or five pounds for a one shilling bet and the lucky kid would shout his friends into the picture show.

Bets were usually made on 'hunches', dreams or on certain visions people happened to see that day. A riddle was given to the bettors after the first draw so that they had time to think about the answer for the evening. Animal names were used instead of numbers and letters. Anyone could be present for the draw to witness that it was conducted properly and in a fair and just way. Another riddle was given after the evening draw for the following mid-day draw.

Every day after the winners were paid, everyone would go outside, talking a mile a minute. You could hear them cursing.

'I should have *pasang* on tiger but no, I changed my mind and put it on rat.'

'I shouldn't have bet. The bank wins all the time, even if only a few people win, there's still plenty of money left in the pool.'

'I shouldn't go there any more. I never win.'

'Yeah. We all say that when we lose but we never learn.'

That didn't stop them for they'd come back the next day for another go. As soon as people saw a chiffa man, a kind of bookie, coming their way, they'd ask, 'What come out? What come out, *Dhari?*' (Meaning what winning animal had been drawn.)

'Horse come out.'

'Anyone catch it? How much it paid?'

'Two pounds. Plenty people catch him. Banker go broke.'

Sometimes nobody caught the winning animal and the chiffa man would say, 'Banker win today. Baldhead Tailor very lucky today. Plenty money go him.'

When our parents hit it big, they'd shout us to the pictures or buy Chinese takeaway for us. We liked it when they had a win because our mob had big hearts when it came to spending. It didn't matter much if they spent all the money in the next few days. I suppose it was just the way it's always been.

It was quite all right to run these games, according to local people, as long as the games were run by Asian people, for Asians only. Naturally enough, that didn't happen. Native people, men and women, as well as a few white gamblers, went there to play cards or Chinese games. The linju turned a blind eye and they hardly interfered with the gambling unless there was a disturbance, which would have to be reported to them. Of course, there were stories regarding gambler's bad luck as well as the good luck stories, especially from the 1920s to the 1940s.

I think that Broome was a spooky place then and a lot of queer things were going on. We were all frightened about the *pourri pourri* that some old Asian men possessed. There were two of whom I was terrified to death. Whenever I happened to pass them on the street or see them outside their houses, I quickly hurried on with eyes fixed on the ground, sometimes running at a trot. For it was said that their pourri pourri was mighty strong. I didn't want to be turned into a green frog or black cat.

There was also an old West Indian man by the name of Con Gill who was around since Adam was a child, I'm sure. Well, he was one old man who had me scared stiff. It was made worse when we were told he had voodoo magic and could hurt us or even kill us if we gave him cheek and that he'd make voodoo dolls of us to do it. When I grew older I saw him as a harmless old man and felt terrible about all those thoughts of those probably innocent men. I must have been one stupid kid all right.

Once, when I was with Tracey Cox, we went to an old Chinese couple's home to visit. Tracey always went there with Aunty Mary and Uncle Phillip who helped the couple a lot by doing housework and odd jobs for them. The couple was very old and frail but managed as well as they could most of the time. The Cox's were kind of like unofficial carers for them.

Anyway, after helping them tidy up things in the house, the old lady offered us some tea and cakes. No worries for Tracey; she just helped herself. I excused myself lamely and watched Tracey finish up, then we left. All the way home I didn't say a thing: I was just staring at her and waiting for her to collapse in a heap. I really thought they were going to poison us. When I told her about my fears a few days later, she just laughed and told me how ridiculous I was. That still didn't change my fears of black magic and voodoo.

There was one story about a player who didn't know much about salang, a modified Asian game based on the stud poker system. He just wanted to play cards. He was told about the rules of the game, which pairs had the higher value, that three of a kind beat doubles and so on. The other gamblers told him that he'd better learn properly first but he insisted on playing, telling them that he knew how to play. Anyway, he played, winning a few, losing a few, until gradually he began losing heavily. By midnight he only had a small stake left. With his last money he played for a huge stake, going all the way to the last card draw. When another player opened the bet on the last card draw, he 'looked' and the other man showed his hand. It was a pair of kings.

'You win. You win,' he said, folded his cards and walked out. He had lost a small fortune. Someone else turned over his folded cards and spread it out for everyone to see what he was chasing. It was the winning hand, a straight hand from seven to jack. They called out to him to come back but he couldn't be seen. About a half hour later, someone went to the men's quarters and found him hanging. He must have thought he had a losing hand.

Some houses held smaller games in the afternoon or evenings and were usually frequented by women and run by a husband and wife team.

Gambling was a livelihood for some families and a pastime for others. My mob's was the former because they had an everyday mission: they had to feed their children as there were no unemployment benefits and no jobs for them. (Only weekly rations were available outside the Native Affairs office.) It was simple Aboriginal logic, play cards then you might win and have money for tucker. You lose, you go home, almost starve and sleep for a week.

At some of the houses, grown-ups played inside while the kids played on a blanket for sixpence and shillings. If any of them went broke, they'd go to their mums crying, 'I want *wanagnurri*. I want wanagnurri.' They'd kick up a big stink, crying and rolling around until they got what they wanted. If their mums were losing, it would be another story and they'd be told to get out or get a good smack on their bottoms for humbugging them.

Aggie, Charlie and I played for money, too. We were pretty smart, though. Yes, we had our fair share of clouts but we learned from experience, if you could call it that. We knew when our mums or aunties were on a winning streak because they'd be in a good mood, laughing and talking, cracking a few jokes here and there or happily yarning away. Money would come flying out of their purses or pockets, loading us with handfuls of coppers and silvers. When they'd ask us to go to the shops to buy smokes, lollies, cool drinks and biscuits, we knew that they were winning and it was time for us to strike. We knew that they'd let us keep the change, too. We also knew when they were losing so most times we steered clear and hid ourselves somewhere else.

When they were playing at Aunty's for big money, Aunty Kudjie would ask one of us to keep an eye out for the linju, in case they got raided. The customers were always treated well and looked after properly. All the players were served food and refreshments, hot cups of tea and coffee, sandwiches and smokes during the games, while the games lasted. Cigarette smoke hung in the air and when it got bad, the shuttered windows were opened to let it out. Sometimes the games lasted for two or three days with people coming and going at different times, just to keep the game alive. It was a pretty good set up for the house-people, for they took commission from every hand that was played. Some people didn't even go home; they just brought their change of clothes, showered up, took a nap, grabbed a bite and got stuck into the game all over again.

There was an old full blood Aboriginal man named Jularu, who lived at Uncle's place, doing odd jobs and helping out with everything. He was a great old man, lean and tall and must have been a very strong man in his youth. We had never seen him angry as he was always grinning away. He minded all of us like a mother hen, telling us story after story about anything and everything. I always thought and took it for granted that he was one of Uncle's people from Sunday Island, for he was treated just like one of the family. I think that it was only a few years ago when uncle told me that he was a Yawuru man. Uncle told us kids a couple of yarns about the gambling days. Some of the stories I can vaguely remember but he told us anyway, from time to time.

Well, one day Jularu was asked to keep an eye out for the linju. That day, he must have been feeling tired for he fell asleep on the job. Before everyone knew it, the linju burst into the room, catching everyone by surprise. There was nothing they could do. They were caught red-handed. You should have seen their faces. The little ones were too busy playing around the yard to notice the linju coming, so they couldn't warn anyone at all.

'Okay, you lot, you're all under arrest! Don't touch the money or cards! You over there? Grab the money and put it in this bag. You and you,' ordered the sergeant, pointing to two women whose names he didn't know, 'pick up the cards and blanket. As for the rest of you, I want you to pick up the chairs and table and start marching to the police station. Hurry up! I've got no time to waste on you lot. You all know it's against the law for you natives to gamble.'

'That bloody Jularu! Anyone seen him? He must've gone looking for *gurry*,' whispered Aunty to no one in particular. She received no reply from the others. They just stared at the four uniformed linju, each one in turn picking up a chair and walking down the steps, silently. Poor fellows, they must have felt no good, especially if they happened to be the losers and not getting a chance to win back their money.

Just down the hill from Kennedy's Store stood the police station to where Uncle, Aunty, my Mimi Alice, my mum and the other gamblers began their long walk. Nearly all of Chinatown rushed out of the shops and houses to look at the strange procession of chairs, table and people. The gamblers were jokingly ribbed about the raid and they joked back to the crowd, in true blackfella style. Even though they may have felt a little ashamed, our mob never really cared. It wasn't the first time they were humiliated. I suppose you could say that they were kind of used to it. They would only be fined and the money and cards confiscated, then their lives would return to the same routine until the next raid. The table and chairs were returned to them (they had to walk back home with the evidence so there was really no need in taking them to the police station in the first place, was there?) It was usually a bad loser or angry husband or wife, looking for their partner, who would have reported the gambling, if only for spite. For days and days everybody was kept busy in trying to guess the identity of the dobber-in.

After they were released on bail and went home, Aunty found old Jularu fast asleep under the house. The house was built on stilts and it was cool underneath when the sea breeze was blowing. They had a good laugh about it when they told Jularu what had happened.

'True God, I never know anything. I been sleeping all the time,' laughed the old man, 'and true God, I wasn't *gurajun*.'

Another time, they were visited by the sergeant and three linju, two of them having just arrived from Perth. Earlier that afternoon, an argument had developed between a man and his wife who had lost money in a game. The man had been drinking and was looking for money to buy more gurry. When told by his wife that she had nothing left, he grew angry and a fight broke out between them and the rest of the gamblers. He accused them all of robbing his wife and cheating her inside out, demanding that the money be returned to her. After an angry exchange of words, he got hunted out of the place by everybody, then must have reported them to the linju, so they reckoned.

Within half an hour, the people heard the kids singing out, 'Yor-yor! Yor-yor! Linju! Linju!' The kids came running back fast to their parents, still pointing to the linju.

They could see that two of the uniformed men were new and must have recently graduated from police training. They had guessed that the two had been brought there to show how they handled any complaints against the natives in Broome. When the gamblers spotted the linju, they quickly grabbed the money and hid it. The linju surveyed the gamblers and the sergeant started questioning them.

'Okay. You mob playing for money?'

'Nah.'

'You got cards there, so what are you playing?'

'Bridge,' replied Mimi Woey, another of Mimi Alice's cousin sisters.

'Don't look like bridge to me. Bloody funny looking bridge

to us, don't you guys reckon?' he asked, turning to the two new blokes. The two looked uncomfortable for they were new to this kind of questioning of native people. In time, though, they'd probably be doing the same kind of things as their mates did and enjoying it, too.

'Well, you mob look like you're playing for money. Don't tell me you're all sitting in a big circle playing for fun? Again I'll ask you what you're playing?'

'It's bridge. You can't see?' answered Mimi Esther, sister to Mimi Woey.

'I didn't know bridge had ten players sitting around in a circle.'

'This is our own bridge. We can play it any way we like to.'

'Okay, one wise woman that you are. Where's the money, then?'

'What money? You guys can't see we got no money here? We're playing for fun. What's wrong with you? You guys supposed to be smart policemen. You supposed to know everything?'

'Okay, okay. Just don't make us come back. You think you're so smart yourself but if I catch you mob playing for money, there'll be hell to pay. I'll run you all in. You hear that?'

They all nodded in silence. As soon as the linju left, they all laughed and laughed for ages, until someone said, 'Who's still playing. Put your money in now.'

'*Jingerose*, Aunty Woey. Where you know bridge from, hey?' Aunty Kudjie asked her.

'Never mind you. I know some tricks. Hey-hey,' she laughed. 'They can go stuff themselves.'

Whether it was playing cards up the hill, known as Indian Territory, down the marsh, at Running Water, the old council yard or wherever they happened to play, our mob always got raided.

COUSIN BONNIE AND AUNTY KUDJIE (KATHLEEN)

There was hardly a dull moment in Broome. If the gambling action wasn't down the marsh, it was on somewhere else around the place. Yes, Aunty and Uncle's place was always full of people coming and going, coming and going. Sometimes, when the gambling down the marsh got slack or died down, our mob went to the other parts of town for a game. The game was often poker but they also played other games. If Uncle didn't drive Aunty and her sisters to the games, they'd grab a taxi and we'd all be loaded into it. The taxi drivers knew everybody, from little kids to old people. They knew where to pick up people and where to drop them off. Passengers didn't have to give an exact address. All they needed was to say, 'Take me to Tommy Taylor's place' or 'Drop me off at Kudjie's place.' The old-time taxi drivers developed a good rapport with our mob in Broome.

Mothers always took their small children with them whenever they went playing cards. Of course, the older kids stayed home or played with friends. They didn't want to be dragged around to gambling houses to mind their little brothers and sisters. Not me, though. I enjoyed being dragged around to those places because I would meet up with friends and we'd have a good time playing hide and seek, chasey, skipping or climbing trees. There'd be occasional fights, with little kids being bullied by the big kids. Mums usually sorted things out but sometimes there'd be arguments between the mums for silly reasons about their kids. Other than that, the outings went well, especially if our mums and aunties happened to be the winners.

Everyone got happy when the luggers came in because they knew the big game of kaja-kaja or four-card would be played at Mr Dep's place. Mr Dep also owned the tailor shop and had a good business. One of Mum's earlier jobs was taking care of their baby Brian some years before.

This was their chance to win big money from the pearling men. The Chinese men and later on, the Japanese, when they were allowed back in the country after the war, were the big-time gamblers and would hold the bank most of the time. To hold the bank, one would have to put money 'up front' to cover the placed bets. Most bankers could declare that the bets would be covered, by stating that they would play 'pocket' money or 'no speak' banker. The players took it on trust that the bankers would cover their bets otherwise all hell would break loose. So they usually played by the rule. Sometimes the game would go on for hours and hours. If the bankers were on a losing streak the word would spread like wildfire. This was a chance for people to win the big money from the Chinese or Japanese. People came from all corners of the town to try their hand. It was like an epidemic catching everyone in its wake.

Children weren't allowed in there but on some occasions, we'd sneak in there to see if our parents were playing, hoping they were winning. Our eyes bulged when we say all the fivers and tenners floating around the table, with the tong box placed near the banker. If bankers were losing the tong box was usually empty. On the other hand, if they were winning, the tong box would be filling up quickly with the commission from the winnings, making Mr Dep a happy man indeed.

Our mob all knew that gambling was illegal and wondered how the Asian dens were allowed to operate. Perhaps the linju turned a blind eye seeing that there were no disturbances or harm being done. Or perhaps they saw the need as recreation for the Asians who had left their families at home overseas and this was one of them. It makes you wonder why they only raided the card games that the natives ran. What was the difference between the Asians who gambled and the natives who gambled?

One of the stories Uncle Jacob told us about was the time he and Ludo Hunter were itchy to play cards but didn't have enough money, so Ludo whipped up a plan. He only had a twenty pound note, a red one like the $20 bill of today. He got a pair of scissors and old newspapers from Uncle and began cutting out rectangle shapes from the money. When he had a pile he took the money and wrapped it around the newspaper notes, folded them in halves and placed them in his white nylon see-through shirtfront pocket, the red note facing outside, looking like he had a big bundle of money in the pocket.

'See what I mean?' said Ludo. 'It looks like I got plenty of money. I'll take banker and you'll be my *bundusang*.'

'You can't do that,' replied uncle. 'They'll catch you.'

'You just watch me. Tell old Jularu to stand by the light switch and when I give the signal by coughing, tell Jularu to turn off the light for a few seconds, then turn it on again. Leave the rest to me. If I got a good hand, there'll be no coughing. Okay?'

When he finally took the bank, he said he would play from the pocket, which meant that he didn't have to show them the actual amount to cover the bets. It was based on trust.

He was lucky that he'd won on the first three hands and didn't have to touch the notes in his pocket. On his very next hand, he didn't look at Uncle or Jalaru; he just coughed. Suddenly, the light went off and there was shouting from the gamblers.

'Ahya! What happened, Jacob? Fix up light quickly. Nobody touch money!'

In seconds, the light was restored and everyone burst out laughing, blaming the powerhouse workers.

This went on for a while during the next few hours until Ludo threw in the bank. He had a good win and split the money with Uncle and Jularu.

'Good job for that mob. They're always cheating us and winning us,' said Ludo. 'It's payback time.'

No one was any the wiser and Ludo never pulled that stunt again.

We loved it when the Asian bankers lost, for it meant that we'd have plenty of food in the house, our mums would have new nylon frocks, maybe we'd also have new frocks, we'd have some spending money and home would be a little brighter and happier. That mood could last for days and days. Of course that didn't mean that our homes weren't happy but only that life was a little easier for a while, with the extra cash in the household.

CHINATOWN

I WAS FORTUNATE TO LIVE IN CHINATOWN. By fortunate, I mean that there was such a conglomeration of nationalities, Chinese, Malayans, Indonesians (mostly Koepangers), Japanese, Ceylonese, Indians, whites and us blacks. I learned that the world was big and people came from far and wide. Not all of them spoke English. They had their own native language and nobody stopped them from speaking it.

By mixing with their children, I learned a little about their lifestyles, their cultures, traditions and religions. I definitely wasn't full bottle on such matters but my friends and I became aware of the different races of people in town. Children notice a lot about people that adults sometimes do not and we are curious enough to ask questions when we see our friends living, speaking and eating differently to us. To this day, I cannot eat with chopsticks and not for want of trying, either.

The native kids in Chinatown, especially us cousins, liked hanging around with the Chinese kids because we knew them from shopping in their stores or just by living in Chinatown. Street kids just naturally hung around with each other. The Chinese kids who were our friends were the Fong kids. They were Glenda, Chester and Phyllis. The other Fong kids were too young to play with us but they still hung around. Everyone called Mr Fong by his first name, Willy, but we always called Mrs Fong just plain Missus. They were very good to us, especially Missus. Whenever we played there, she'd feed us till we were bursting at the seams. Chinese food sure was heaven! She was a good friend to most of the women there, always chatting and yarning to them in the shop or on the shop-front porch. We felt very sad when Missus went away to Melbourne to live. I never saw her again but her son David came back out west some years later and I met him in Port Hedland, where he settled with his own family.

Just around the corner from where we lived, were the Chinese shops and the Sun Picture theatre. The most frequented shop was the famous Ah Ming's Store or Anawai's, the same Anawai who travelled to Beagle Bay with our mob. He still let people book up goods and food in his shop. They'd fix him up on paydays, endowment days or if they happened to win in cards. We'd book up lollies, biscuits and soft drinks to our parents, so whenever we were hungry, we'd head for Anawai's. We'd go on a spending spree, shouting our little mates. If it was stone fruit season, we'd book up big mobs of apricots, plums, peaches, grapes or whatever else was available. Sometimes we'd overspend our limit but the bill was paid promptly. Of course, we'd take some of the goodies home for the smaller kids. Our parents were satisfied as long as we didn't buy smokes, like some of the other kids did. Even though we could book up, there were others who couldn't so they played tricks on poor old Anawai.

One trick amongst those kids was covering the pennies with silver paper to make them look like two bob pieces. One kid would bang on the counter with the fake two bob calling out, 'Anawai! Anawai! I wanna buy olangee. You got any olangee? Hully up! Hully up!' making him come up to the front counter. Most times he'd be down the back, counting his money. As he'd come shuffling up one aisle, a couple of kids would sneak down another aisle and start filling their pockets with goodies or they'd grab a couple of bottles of soft drinks or biscuits or whatever else they could grab for a feed. The kid up the front kept Anawai busy by haggling about the prices of different food lines or the size and quantity of the fruit.

'This olangee too small. Gimmee a big one, Anawai.'

As he shuffled down the back of the shop, the other kids would sneak up the front and out the door. When he'd get back to the counter, the kid would pay him with the fake coin and he'd put it in the drawer without even checking it. That seemed to work most of the time. Other times when he woke up to the tricks, he'd say, 'You kids plopper no good. I catchee, I tell mummy and daddy.'

On odd occasions he managed to catch some of the kids stealing and would whack them with a straw broom or stick that he kept handy.

No one thought of it as stealing even though our parents warned us not to try those tricks on anyone, especially old Anawai as he was good to our mob. We knew who the kids were but never dobbed them in. It was just a game. Whenever Anawai found out who the little culprits were, he'd tell their parents about it and duly charge them. They were never reported to the police. The kids got reprimanded by their parents, time and time again but as they got older, they stopped doing it. By that time, I suppose, they must have thought there was no fun left in it. They were no longer kids.

In a nutshell, I guess we were all guilty because none of us knocked back a drink or biscuit from the kids.

Poor old Anawai. Sometimes we'd call out to him chanting, 'Anawai, run away, this way, that way.' It would go on repeatedly, with us bursting out laughing, every time. He'd come out shouting, 'What you want? What you want?'

'You got flootee? You got olangee, plummee, glapee? Gimmee lolly, Anawai. Please, Anawai. We'll pay you tomollow.'

Sometimes he'd humour us by standing there and waving his stick around as if to shoo us out of his shop. Other times, he'd walk away, shaking his head, taking no notice. We must have made him sick. Poor old Anawai. We hadn't thought of the teasing as giving cheek, we were just clowning around.

We hung around another old Chinaman who was called Ah Kim, the long soup man. We'd go over to his long soup shop and talk to him, watching him make his noodles and satays for the evening rush. We were fascinated with his cutting machine and would watch him for ages, hanging out the long strands to dry. We'd beg him for the leftover dough to play, making dough dolls and animal shapes. We'd talk to him asking all sorts of questions but he'd just keep nodding and smiling. I don't think he understood a word we said. On the other hand, he may have been too clever for us and just played dumb.

We all agreed that he made the best long soup in the world and no one could beat Ah Kim and his wonderful long soup. Just about once a week, we'd go over and have long soup and satays, otherwise Aunty Kudjie would send old Jularu to get takeaway. If we helped him during the day during school holidays or on Saturdays, he promised us free long soup. On those nights, we made sure that we all turned up in full force. None of us wanted to miss out on his long soup.

People said he made satays from stray cats in Chinatown but we didn't believe the stories because we watched him prepare the satays and helped him skewer the meat, which he bought from the butcher shop every morning. Anyway, cats are too boney to have much flesh to make satays.

There were no playgrounds or designated recreation areas in town, only the old vacant, dilapidated prewar buildings, the marsh and the foreshores, our own houses, the backyards of the Chinese parents' shops and the streets. Their parents must have felt sorry for us by giving us heaps to eat when we played over there. We didn't feel offended by it; we thought it was just great. Chinese food was heaven and we loved it. Most of their parents owned restaurants or small general stores and were considered wealthy by our standards. They also knew our parents very well, because a good many of them played cards together and gambled their money and time away. Just about everybody knew everybody.

A Chinese couple, the Jan's, also owned an ice-cream shop in Chinatown. We thought it was the next best thing to an American soda shop, with servings of banana splits, milkshakes and shaved ice cordials in tall glasses. The only thing lacking was a jukebox. We hung out there whenever we had heaps of money. Later when we moved to Robinson Street, we walked to Jan's at least twice a week and in the really hot weather we practically ran there after school just to drink the shaved ice cordials until we cooled off.

As well as the two general stores, Streeter & Male and Kennedy & Sons that faced each other at opposite ends of Chinatown, there were a couple of Indian or Ceylonese shops, Chinese shops and restaurants, the usual bakery and butchers, a hotel, an old ice factory and the Sun Pictures theatre. There were two more hotels, a couple of stores, the Native Hospital, the District Hospital, the two schools and the meatworks on the port side of town. I related more to Chinatown in my early years, and it wasn't until I was about ten that we moved to the other side of Broome.

We all relied on the ice factory for the daily ice blocks because we didn't have a kerosene or electric refrigerator in those days. Uncle only had an old icebox or an old Coolgardie fridge in the house and so it had to do for us. If any of our uncles or old Jularu couldn't pick up the ice block in the morning, we had to push

CARNARVON ST, CHINATOWN, 1950s
LtoR: ANAWEI'S, TACK'S, WING'S AND SUN PICTURES.

an old cane pram that didn't have any rubber tyres, all the way up the streets till we got to the place. Then we'd have to push the pram all the way back. Sometimes we'd get talking to friends or start playing marbles with them, forgetting all about the ice melting in the pram. Oh well, better to have half an ice block than none at all. Other times when we got sidetracked and saw Uncle Jacob or Uncle Johnny Hunter heading for us, we'd jump up and start running full speed with the old pram, trying to dodge him, calling out, 'We're coming Uncle. We're coming.'

Even when we were sent to get bread, we'd do stupid things. The fresh hot bread smelt wonderful, especially the golden crust. Walking home, we'd start picking at the smaller side of the bread and eat it little by little, making a small hole, gradually hollowing it out to the centre. By the time the bread reached home there was hardly any of the insides left. We'd either get a good ear bashing or ear clipping, depending on their mood. They had said that if we had stinging ears, we might listen properly. On top of that we had to walk all the way back for more loaves. If the bread was sold out we had to be satisfied to eat damper or pancakes.

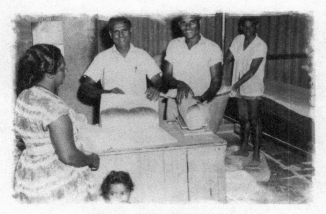

MUM, WITH MARGY, BUYING BREAD.
LtoR: UNCLE PHILLIP COX, UNCLE MATTHEW COX, UNCLE FREDDY COX

There were a number of living quarters in town for the pearling crews. They were built near the foreshores and in close proximity to the pearling companies' moorings. The quarters were known by the individual company's name such as Streeter camp, Morgan camp and McDaniel camp and the likes. The camps accommodated the different groups of Asian men employed by the pearling companies for their seamanship and their diving skills and knowledge of the ocean.

They nearly all lived in close comfort to each other, a little too close, I'd imagine. It seemed that the white pearling masters did not consider the diversely cultural, religious and traditional differences of each group. They chucked them in one 'hot pot' probably thinking that all Asian men are the same and that they'd be happy just sharing the living quarters.

That wasn't the case in the 1920s when there was a bloody feud between the Japanese and Koepangers and the fighting went on for days. There was also a feud between the Malayans and Koepangers in the 1930s. The only way to distinguish them apart was for the Koepangers to paint white 'armbands' onto their upper arms. Apparently the same armbanding had been done to distinguish the two races in the Japanese clash.

Later on after the Second World War, there were some improvements in the accommodation arrangements for the men, and socially, things turned out for the better.

We played down the alleyways, up the hill: never gave a hang where we played. We knew old Chinatown inside out and off by heart. The old vacant and dilapidated houses in town were part of our playing areas. Most were boarded up and securely locked but there were some that we played in because they were open, somehow. Others were occupied by squatters. We were constantly told not to play near or in them because of the dangers of old buildings, the rotting timbers and whatever else. They also told us not to go peeping through the windows because some houses still had paintings, mostly of naked Chinese concubines, hanging on the walls. We sort of knew about the nude paintings because Sally and some of the other girls actually saw them when they went stickybeaking all right. Our eyes must have been bigger than two-bob pieces. We had never seen the likes of such pictures. Our little hearts were pounding with shock and shame. We should not have disbelieved our mums who knew everything.

'Wadda gee. They got no shame. We'd better go back and don't you guys ever tell our mums about this, okay?'

After that one time of peeping, we were too frightened and ashamed to go back and have another look. I don't know whether the rightful owners ever claimed them and I don't really want to know. Not one of us ever told our mums about that incident and we carried that secret guilt in our hearts for years and years.

❖

Another thing that fascinated me was the scene in Chinatown that occurred every evening. After siesta time, the town would slowly awaken to the sounds of afternoon trading and by five o'clock when the major businesses were closing up, the Chinatown nightlife started. People began gathering around the shop fronts and verandahs, waiting for the Chinese restaurants to open or to go shopping for forgotten items because the shops were open until eight or nine o'clock for night trading, or perhaps getting ready for gambling.

There were mixed races of people talking to each other, singing or shouting out from across the shops on the opposite side. The main group was the Chinese people because they had shops right in the centre of town and lived there with their families. One group would begin outside Anawai's, another outside Tang Wei's and Tack's and some would just stand there in the middle of the street, openly discussing the events of the day or their overseas home news, I suppose. Anyway, the racket would go on and on, getting louder and louder by the minute. Even old Mrs Dep and Mrs Fong would walk halfway across and join in the discussions, gesturing with arms and hands or stand there with arms akimbo

It was no big deal for us to witness those daily scenes for they had been part of Chinatown culture and had been going on long before my time. The native people just minded their own business and discussed their own affairs in their own way so they never took heed of the Chinese people's daily gatherings. Then around six or seven o'clock the Chinese crowd would slowly disperse and go home or make their way to the *chiffa* draw.

Then one day, just out of the blue, the linju suddenly

converged upon them in their paddy wagon, trying to keep calm and control the crowd, trying to find out what was going on.

'Nothing. Nothing. We only talk Chinese business. No trouble. No trouble.'

Apparently, a couple of strangers to the town, probably tourists, had witnessed this normal behaviour and jumped to the conclusion that an Asian melee was about to happen. So they panicked and reported the 'uprising' to the linju who duly acted on it. The crowd quickly dispersed and all was quiet again.

THE THINGS GIRLS DO

AGGIE AND I LOVED PLAYING DRESS-UPS in our mums' and aunties' clothes and shoes. Sometimes we painted ourselves silly with red lipstick and powder. Living in town sort of changed the lives of our mums, mimis and aunties a little bit and for many of the mission girls. Not drastically but in small ways, which I had failed to notice in my youth. The young women in Beagle Bay took pride in their appearances because of the teachings of the missionaries. It was not done in a vain way but because they were taught that 'cleanliness is next to Godliness' and that reflected on their teachings. They just wanted to feel and smell beautiful.

The young native people who were brought up in towns such as Broome and Derby were more exposed to the fashion world than the mission girls and many of them were smart dressers. It seemed that society was a little kinder, or a bit more tolerant that in previous times, for some of our young people had more employment opportunities than our mothers and grandmothers. They were able to help their families, have a few bob to spend and go out to picture shows and dances. They were still an oppressed or suppressed people in whatever way one may look at it but things seemed a little better on the surface.

There was also the Asian influence on the native society which had a great impact during Broome's heyday. Because of the Asian people's employment with the pearlers, there were goods that they could acquire easily. Many of these goods were also enjoyed by native people through intermarriages or relationships and genuine friendship.

The kids of Chinatown were a mixture of Chinese, Ceylonese, Malaysian, Koepangers, Japanese, whites, full bloods, half-castes and quarter-castes from either white, native or Asian parents. Most of the white kids had white mothers who lived with either Indonesians or Koepangers. Their mothers became known as the 'Melbourne women'. Most of the Melbourne women seemed nice and friendly and got along well with the native women who also took Asians for their husbands or partners. It was said that those women came from poor families or broken-down marriages and had followed those men to Broome for a safer and better lifestyle. Perhaps the idea of living in a flourishing pearling town in the tropics infatuated them. Broome must have sounded very romantic to them. For sure, it must have been better than living in a cold, wet climate, especially if you were poor. Then again, they must have loved their men to come all the way up to Broome. I couldn't imagine any white person being poor like us but they must have been, obviously.

The white kids of the Melbourne women were okay I suppose and a little older than us in age. I found out through playing with some of those girls, who had Koepanger fathers. They had plenty of clothes, shoes, toys and most of all, they had lots and lots of jewellery, precious stones such as diamonds and rubies, real gold chains, real gold rings, pendants, bracelets, brooches and ear-rings. So did their mums! Our eyes popped wide when we first saw such fine jewellery. We only saw such things in treasure troves in the picture shows, not in people's homes.

One of those girls, Betty Marwon, used to let us play with her toys and dress up in her and her mum's clothes, hats and shoes. We'd put on our make-up, having learned a little from our aunties of course and prance around with Mrs Marwon's high-heeled shoes. We thought we looked gorgeous. Up and down the stairs we'd go, pretending we were film stars.

Betty was a big girl for her age. She was very white for a child who had a dark Koepanger for her dad, so she must have followed her mum in colouring and her dad in her Asian looks.

On more than one occasion, she let Aggie and me wear her jewels around the house. She had to be very careful with them, her mum stressed more than once. We played all that day, dressing up in her clothes and fine jewels. I tried on Betty's gold ring and it was a bit snug but I still wore it.

In the afternoon, we had a feed, changed back into our own clothes, then started to head home. On the way out, I was about to take off the ring when Betty said that I could mind it for her and bring it back the next day. At teatime, I began to feel a twinging pain in my hand and noticed a little swelling around the finger. Aggie and I went to the bathroom sink to soap my hand and try to get the ring off but no go. We decided not to tell Mum, because she might make us walk back in the dark to return it.

It was a fair walk to Betty's house and the way my finger was hurting only made me want to go to sleep, hoping the pain would somehow disappear. I thought there was no real need to tell Mum about the ring hurting me, but it didn't quite turn out that way. Later that night my finger swelled up so bad that I was in sheer agony and I went crying to her, showing her my swollen finger where the ring almost cut into my flesh. She also tried in vain to get it off with soap and water but to no avail. Finally she took me to old Mr Ellies, the jeweller, who had to cut off the ring. She had to go around the back, banging on the door, for it was well after closing time. It was relief for my finger but not for me. I had to tell Mum that Betty let me wear the ring until the next day when we'd go back to play with her again.

'You're lucky not to have your finger cut off, you silly girl,' she said. 'Talk about shame, waking up old Mr Ellies in the middle of the night. You're lucky that it's too dark and too late to take you to Mrs Marwon. It's bad enough that we had to wake the old man. I don't know what old Mrs Ellies is going to say when she sees me at the shop.'

Next morning, she took me to Mrs Marwon, making me explain everything to her. Mum made me apologise as well, then she offered to have the ring repaired. Somehow, Mrs Marwon told us not to worry about it, that she'd pay for it herself. She said that I could still play with Betty but no more playing with jewellery. Maybe Mrs Marwon felt sorry for Mum and me, because by this time I had a stepfather, Ala Dia. He was a Koepanger, just like her husband and those countrymen were a tight-knit group. Those people respected each other and Mum must have felt no good about the whole thing, thanks to me. She said that I made her and Dad feel shame. It made me feel no good either, even though Aggie and I knew that it was a mistake to mind it for the night. We had no idea about the face value of the ring, only that it was so pretty. A couple of years later, Betty left Broome for good, to live in Melbourne with her mother. We sure missed Betty Marwon and all her finery!

AGNES AND ALA'S WEDDING, BROOME 1956

Oh yes, most of the pretty young town girls were smart dressers and smart lookers, all right. They dressed up for work or just to go down the streets to shop or to the picture show. I think Hollywood pictures and America itself influenced Australians at large and perhaps the rest of the world as well.

My Mimi Alice herself dressed so handsomely in her best clothes, handbag, hat, ear-rings and brooch, which she wore on special days. She kept all her things in one place and no one was allowed to touch them. It was her little things that she valued, even though they were simple. What she did have was only costume jewellery and her pearl but she treasured them like they were the Jewels of the Nile or the keys to the Kingdom of Heaven.

Mimi picked up her dress sense from the society ladies for whom she worked, for she had to lay out their clothing from day to day, which hat and shoes to wear with which dress, nothing loud, not too many jewellery pieces, just the simple but elegant style except, of course, when they threw lavish garden parties and held balls.

Aggie and I always watched in fascination as our aunties Bella and Binyu applied Pond's cleansing cream to their faces, working it into their skins then rubbing it off with cotton wool. After that, they'd apply the Pond's vanishing cream then lightly powder-puff their faces with talc. As they finally applied the red lipstick, our little mouths opened and pressed together, as though the lipstick was on our own lips. After that, splash, splash, splash went their favourite scent behind their ears, on their necks and wrists. They'd give themselves a final look in the mirror and then they'd be off to town.

Our two aunties had left Beagle Bay and for a time lived in

the Convent hostel for working girls. I cannot remember much of their time in the hostel only on the mission and in Chinatown down the marsh. During this time they were single girls but married a few years later. Aunty Bella became Mrs Ronny Walker and Aunty Binyu became Mrs Johnny Hunter. Yes, they did marry in church.

One day when our aunties went out, Aggie and I had to stay with Mum and Mimi Alice. We went into the aunties' room and spotted all the goodies on the dressing table. We started to open the jars and bottles to smell the contents, when quickly replaced the lids. We didn't know much about face creams and make-up, only from what we saw our aunties doing. After a while, I reached for a small jar and began putting the cream on my face. I tried to work it into my face, doing what my aunties had done. I then put on the lipstick, a little crooked but it looked okay, I suppose. Before I had time to put on the powder, I heard the door open and then a shocked cry from my mum.

'Goodness gracious, girl! What's wrong with your face? Look at you! Just look at you! You look like I don't know what! What did you put on yourself, hey? Come here and have a look at yourself.'

She grabbed me by the back of my head and marched me to the mirror. I didn't look at the mirror straight away but grabbed the small jar and showed it to her.

'I only put on Aunty's face cream, and…and…and…a little bit lipstick.'

'No wonder,' she said, taking the jar and forcing me to look at myself in the mirror. 'This is deodorant cream, not face cream. That's why your face is still white and sticky. Does your armpit look like your face? You're gonna just tell your aunties what you did. Hear me?' Then she had a good go trying to scrub it off.

Of course, I had to tell my aunties. Every now and again one of them would laugh and call out to me, 'Heh-hey. Wanna have another go, Betty-girl?' They thought it was funny, all right.

Another time, I was watching Aunty Bella splash some scent on herself from a big bottle of eau de cologne. She dabbled a little on my throat, too. It felt so cool and smelt so lovely. When she left the room, I looked longingly at the bottle, wanting to open it and smell its perfume again. After a few minutes, I gave into temptation, opened the bottle and breathed in deeply. It smelled so beautiful, so beautiful that I just had to see if it tasted as beautiful as it smelt. I soon found out! It knocked the wind out of me and spun me to the floor. It stung my tongue and mouth and went right up my nose. It felt like fire and I could hardly breathe. I ran screaming outside to Aunty Kudjie, pointing to my mouth. She grabbed me then smelt the strong perfume on me. She quickly chucked me into the wash trough and poured clean tap water into my mouth. Aunty Bella came running from the front of the house to see was going on as soon as she heard the screams. Once again I had to tell them what a stupid thing I had done.

'Did you ever see me and your aunties drink bottles of scent, hey? Ask first if you want to find out things. Okay?' said Aunty Kudjie. 'You used to ask us before, so how come you never did this time? I don't know what jidja Aggie will say when I tell her about this?'

They couldn't stop laughing at me even when they saw the tears rolling down my cheeks. I couldn't blame them for I brought it on myself.

I will never forget that taste for the rest of my life, that's for sure. Kids do stupid things in their young lives whether on impulse, deliberately or for a dare. Most times they do it, not realising it's stupid and wrong, for their foolish acts could injure or hurt other people and themselves for that matter.

I wasn't the only one who did silly things. Towards the end of 1952, when Aggie was eight and I was ten, all the shops started to display their Christmas goodies: toys, bikes, hampers and numerous wares. For weeks and weeks, as Aggie and I passed Streeter's store on the way to little jetty, we always stopped to admire the window dressing and the ladies bike that was on display. It was indeed a beautiful rainbow-coloured bike, the first we had ever seen in our lives. It was the only one of its kind in Broome. We both bagsed it from the very first day that we saw it. Every time we approached the store, we'd have a bet to see if it was still there, desperately wishing that nobody had bought it yet. It was priced at forty-five pounds.

From that first day, Aggie said to me, 'I'm gonna have that bike for Christmas. I'm gonna ask my papa to buy me that bike. I'm gonna humbug him for it every day. I'm gonna humbug him every day until he gives in.'

So humbug him she did. I knew that she had a good chance of getting that bike because Uncle had regular work and he was very lucky in cards. I still bagsed it though but I'd be happy just to have a go on it. So, everyday Aggie pestered her dad.

'Where are we gonna get money for it? We have to wait until money come in,' was his usual reply.

'Yeah, but can I buy it?' asked Aggie.

'Oh yeah, you can buy,' said Uncle, who knew that she didn't have any money and was unable to buy it, anyway. He chuckled to himself, giving Aunty a sign with his eyes and mouth.

A few days before Christmas, Aggie and I again went to Streeter's. It was still there. She went over to a lady, whose name I can't remember and said, 'My papa said I can buy that bike for Christmas. That rainbow-coloured bike over there. You can book it up to him. His name is Jacob Sesar and he works for Mr Streeter and Mr Male.'

Everyone at Streeter's knew Uncle and so it was all fixed up. Across the marsh Aggie flew, little legs pumping, standing up because she couldn't reach the saddle, and with me running behind her. As usual, the mob was sitting on the ground outside playing cards. Someone called out 'El-double-o, Kudjie. Look! Aggie's riding here on a new bike.' They all turned around and stared at this little girl on a big bike, little legs pedalling away. She pulled up short next to Uncle, grinning from ear to ear.

'Look papa! Look papa! I got a bike. I got a rainbow bike and it's all mine.'

'Where you got it from, Aggie?' asked Uncle. 'I booked it up at Streeter's. You said I could buy it, remember?' 'I only said if we had money. That's all.'

'Yeah, Jacob, you did say it,' said Aunty. 'More you like to tell her. See what happened now? You can just go and see that mob at Streeter's now and fix it up. You hear?'

So he had to go to Streeter's and sort it out. Aggie kept the bike, all right, that beautiful rainbow-coloured bike. It was Aggie's pride and joy. I'd say that it was the pride and joy of Chinatown. Eventually, it was ridden into the ground by all the kids of Chinatown, but we sure had fun doing it.

WATER

ON WEEKENDS OR HOLIDAYS, we'd beg our parents to go swimming down at Bathing Shed Beach at big jetty (now known as Town Beach). Big jetty was taboo for us without grown-ups. Our parents had to take us there or we'd have to go there with other family members or with trusted people. We were never allowed to go there on our own, at our age. We were told about that time and time again.

'No!' Mum said. 'It's too far away and no one big will be there to look after you kids. If you want to go swimming, go to Streeter jetty. At least there'll be plenty of people and countrymen to watch out for you. What if you guys drown there, hey?'

Streeter jetty was the jetty that the luggers used for re-fuelling, picking up stores and equipment, minor repairs or when the crew got off for shore leave or sick leave. During lay-up season, the jetty became very busy, with people dashing to and fro, kids on bikes, with their dogs following behind and the traffic on the move, with their horns beeping everybody off the road. Lay-up time was when the pearling fleet 'laid up' or closed down at the end of the pearling season, around December, starting again around February for a whole new season.

There'd be men carrying out maintenance work on the laid-up luggers, men working in the shell shed sorting and stacking the shells into packing crates, or just laughing and talking amongst themselves. Despite the language barriers in some instances, they seemed to communicate well enough with each other.

Even though the Streeter jetty swimming area had lots of sea snakes swimming around, we still swam there. You think you'd catch me swimming down there these days? Never!

I liked swimming down there because that was where most of the Chinatown kids hung out. That didn't mean I didn't like going to the big jetty to swim. Anyway, we swam, fished or just fooled around there, diving off the jetty, jumping onto the dinghies or made sandcastles on the beach. Sometimes we went onto the luggers as well, because some of the men who worked there were either our dads or relatives and they rowed us around in the dinghies like they were theirs. Other times they took us kids onto the luggers to have a feed with them. It wasn't much, usually biscuits and tea, sweetened with Nestle condensed milk, or just bread and honey, or maybe some rice and curried corned beef hamper. Then they'd give us some fruit and cordial drinks.

We never felt scared of the people who worked there. They may have been a mixture of races but to us they were just people like anybody else. If our mob could work with them out at sea, then they must have been okay. They all worked together, spoke a common language, which was Malay and just got on with their work. Just about everybody spoke Malay because it was an easy language to pick up. Some of our native men spoke it quite

PEARLING LUGGER, 1958

fluently and would be considered multilingual today, speaking several Asian languages and other native languages as well as good old English. It was a good, simple life and everybody lived it that way. Well, so we all thought.

Even when the tide went out, we stayed on, playing in the mangroves, looking for *bugul-bugul*, sea snakes or cockles. Of course, we went home before it got too dark because we were frightened of the goomboons, hairy, scary, stumpy creatures who lived in the mangroves and just loved to eat children.

One day during the lay-up, my cousins from Port Hedland, Robin and Peter Clarke, Aggie, Charlie and I went to the little jetty for a swim. It was big tide too, which was even better for swimming. We were diving and swimming around, running in and out of the water and onto the beach and back again into the water, which we did for most of the morning, until I got tired and sat down for as spell. The others kept on swimming and enjoying themselves but I just looked on, sort of daydreaming, I suppose. The tide was coming in fast and before I knew it, the planks on the jetty were under water. It must have been a foot above the jetty, probably a king tide.

After about twenty minutes, I noticed some bigger kids diving off the jetty, swimming under it and surfacing out the other end. It looked easy and I decided that I'd have a go. I could swim and hold my breath under the water, just as good as the others. Easy, I told myself. I then ran back and jumped into the water. I took a deep breath and dived beneath the jetty which was still under water. About halfway through, I thought that I was already on the other end so I began to surface. As I was going up, my head struck the planking and I panicked. I tried to duck again and swim a further distance to surface but I kept striking the planks. My little lungs were almost bursting with pain and I kept saying in my mind, 'I'm drowning! I'm drowning! Please God, save me!'

It seemed like a millions years that I was down there. I was kicking and waving my arms about like a madman. I was threshing around in frenzy, still stuck under the planks. Suddenly, I felt these big hands and arms around me, pulling me away and upwards. I was breathless and gasping for air, crying hysterically and falling down on the sand like a limp rag.

'You right, Betty? You right?' a man's voice asked me. I could only nod. My cousins gathered around me quickly for they had witnessed the dramatic rescue, not realising that the victim was me until I was dragged from the water.

When I calmed down, I could see that it was Uncle Raphael Clement who had spoken to me. He said he was watching us swimming and playing around while he was taking a break with the other men to have a smoke. He watched me dive under the jetty and when he saw that I didn't come up, he raced down the beach and dived into the water to look for me. He could see my little body threshing about, grabbed me and pulled me out, never mind the salt water stinging his eyes. That was a close shave indeed. After that one and only time, I never dared try that stunt again. It frightened the daylights out of me, that's for sure.

Thank God for people who watch over little kids. If it wasn't for Uncle Raphael, I wouldn't be here to write this story. We still swam there though but with caution. Life would have been pretty dull without Streeter jetty and yes, we all stopped copying the big kids with their diving tricks.

After lay-up, it was time to go out to sea again and every one of the luggermen would ready the luggers for the long season ahead. The whole town looked forward every year for the lugger races between the pearling companies because family and friends were invited on board with feasting and drinking, jumping overboard to swim in the ocean, until it was time to go ashore. Such wonderful halcyon days they were.

When we weren't allowed to go swimming at the big jetty, we had to settle for the little jetty, more or less. We were quite happy with that rule so we'd make our way to the little jetty and swim around for a little while, until someone mentioned the magic words, big tide and big jetty.

'Hey, you guys. There's a big tide and everyone will be at big jetty. I bet Doris and Sally mob will be at the bathing shed.' Doris Mathews, Maureen Howard and Sally Demin were my close friends (and relations).

'They must be. They always go there at big tide.'

'And guess what? There's a big steamer at the jetty, too. Let's go and see if it's still there. We can go swimming and when the

THE *DULVERTON* AT LOW TIDE ON THE OLD JETTY, 1958

tide goes out we can see the big steamer sitting on the mud. What you guys reckon?'

'Mummy will growl us,' said one of the little kids. We all looked at each other rather slackly but all we needed was a little prompting from someone and off we'd go like a flash. All we could think of was our friends and the good times we'd have over there. We didn't wait for our bathers to dry; we'd just pull on our tops and shorts over them and away we'd go. Our mothers' heeding was forgotten.

'Let's go, you guys, before the tide goes out!'

We couldn't go to the big jetty by way of the town streets because one of our mob was sure to spot us heading that way. We had to walk the long way around by the foreshore, which would have taken us about half an hour to get to the big jetty, judging by our little legs. So on our way there we'd tell stories or just talked our way there, to keep our minds off the long walk ahead. Sometimes the boys would spear the mullet and long toms for bait, in case they decided to fish instead. They made their three-pronged spears from locally grown bamboo and scraps of wire found around the place and tested them down the marsh or little jetty. They stuck their gut lines, which were wound around very short mangrove sticks, and their hooks and sinkers in their pockets or elastic waistbands.

When we'd get to the forbidden place, we'd start running along the beach, pulling off our tops and shorts and jubul straight into the beautiful, cold blue sea with our bathers. We'd come up for air, looking for Doris and Sally or other friends. As soon as they were spotted, we'd swim over to them. Sometimes, we couldn't see them at first, because of all the little black heads bobbing up and down in the water.

Time and reason were lost to us. We'd swim the length and

breadth of the semi-circled, shark-proof swimming enclosure. We'd swap news and gossip, make fun of our 'enemies' or watch the teenagers skite around for their boyfriends and girlfriends.

When we'd arrive at the end of the jetty, there was hustle and bustle, pushing and shoving, lumpers yelling abuse to each other and us getting in the way of everyone. We'd watch the passengers come down the gangway with their small luggage, umbrellas unfolded to ward off the harsh sunlight, young children pulling their mother's skirts, looking frightened and babies laughing, happy to get off the ship, I'm sure.

Sometimes we'd recognise local people on the ships, coming home from their annual holidays. Or new faces that would become familiar over the next few months, bank Johnny's families or families of the Postmaster General and government departments. Usually, the pearling masters took their families down to Perth by ship and returned by the same token. It was such a status thing for them, travelling first class on the passenger ships. It wasn't as if there were no airline services available. It was just the 'done thing' for them to do.

Even if there was a chance for me to travel long distances by a passenger ship, I'd never do it. I had the opportunity once to go aboard a passenger ship on a tour with other school children and was not impressed. Everything was closing in on me when we were taken down to the cabins. They were too small and the rolling of the ship made me sick. I was glad to get out. Yet I loved sailing on the luggers and rowing in the dinghies. Perhaps it was only the claustrophobic experience of going into the interior bowels of the larger vessel.

The best times were when the crew called out to us and started throwing us fruit by the bucketful: apples, oranges, bananas, pears and whatever else they had. There'd be a mad frenzy, white kids and black kids pushing each other around, vying for the goodies. We'd all share the fruit around then go and eat them under the jetty's platform below. It's a wonder no one fell into the sea. There were lots of big sharks hanging around there. We appreciated the fruit and sure, maybe the crew did get a kick out of us scrambling about and maybe they did feel sorry for us, but who cared? Fruit was fruit in any kid's books, and we weren't going to knock them back.

There was one public telephone box on the wharf and we'd scrape up a few pennies to call anyone who had a phone at home. Sometimes we'd just chat to the telephonist or coax her into putting us through for free. We'd tell her that we'd pay her back next week but next week never came. I think she knew that we had no money and just humoured us for being kids.

When we got bored of swimming and were energetic enough, we'd head for the Red Cliff and start walking to Gantheaume Point, a long distance away. Once there, though we'd forget about the distance and time we spent walking to get there and we'd just lose ourselves in combing the beach and rocky outcrops. If the tide was out we'd go looking for trapped fish in the pools or for shells or anything else. I think that I must have done that trip about four or five times in my young lifetime.

Even the foul smell from the meatworks did not deter us from walking to the Point. When the smell hung around the town for days, I'd get sick with vomiting and headaches. Someone said it was the blood and bones burning for making fertiliser. Every time I opened a can of dog pet food, I'd think of the meatworks smell and get sick. It reminded me of burnt blood.

When it was time for us to go home, we weren't so cheerful, knowing that we'd cop it when we got home. We could never lie when asked where we had been. It was pointless anyway because they always knew when we disobeyed them. They must have seen it in our eyes or had some sixth sense or something. Or they were just down right clever.

We'd start crying even before we reached home, before we'd even get our toes into the door. We'd all get a swift whack on the backs of our skinny legs, one by one. We dared not run away from the punishment because we'd only cop it harder when we got caught. It must have been a funny sight all right. With all of us yelling 'Mummy, Mummy, Mummy' in turns, holding onto their skirts and running round and round them, in circles.

SUN
PICTURES

ALL KINDS OF PEOPLE WENT to the picture shows at the Sun Pictures theatre in Broome. It was the only type of wholesome entertainment available at the time and most Saturday nights the place was packed out. It opened its doors to the public in 1916 and is reputed to be the oldest open-air theatre in the world. All I know is that it was still standing strong in 1946 when I was in HCO. My mum and Mimi Alice used to go to the pictures when they first left the mission before the war.

My Aunty Bella, Aunty Binyu and Mimi Alice took me to my first show. I don't know what the film was about but I remember staring at the walls lined with framed black and white photographs of old-time film stars. They looked so old fashioned in their twenties and thirties fashion designs but still looked absolutely stunning. They were just beautiful. I stood there mesmerised on the spot until Aunty Binyu pulled me away to go inside.

Up near the front of the huge silver screen were rows of wooden garden seats for the children. Right behind them were rows of canvas deck chairs and they formed the open-air section of the theatre. Then further back, under the cover of the high ceiling roof was where the Broome society people sat in their reserved 'directors' chairs' type of seating. On either sides of the reserved society seating were more canvas deck chairs for the 'second class' non-natives and the 'better blacks' of the town. They were separated by aisles running the length of the theatre. Then there was the seating for ordinary people in general, where my family usually sat.

Way down the back and away from the central seating was a section of the theatre for full blood natives only. It was like a horse corral, fended off with only a wooden gate to let them get in and out. They had to sit on backless benches in a small, overcrowded area. I didn't know why the full blood natives had to sit down at

SUN PICTURES, 1950s

the back in the cordoned-off area. It just didn't look right, didn't make sense even to a little child like me. They looked like the negro slaves depicted in the Deep South of America films. I asked Mimi Alice why it was so. I had noticed some of my family sitting there, as well.

'How come them mob gotta sit there?'

'I don't know, but they got their own rules, looks like. They've always sat there for as long as I can remember. No one questions white people. You'll know soon enough.'

'But how come we don't sit there, then?'

'Oh, they just don't let us sit there. They only let half-caste people sit outside and only in certain places. It must be because we got a bit of light colour. Don't ask me stupid questions that I don't know how to answer.'

I didn't insist on sitting with my full blood mimis that time but went to sit with my aunties because I was so excited to see my first show. Halfway through the show, I must have fallen asleep because the next thing I knew, I awoke in my bed.

I grew up to love the pictures, or movies, and I went there

every chance I got. I wasn't allowed to go every picture night, which was only three times a week, but could go on Saturday nights with family members or if there was a good show on the odd Thursday night. Of course, as I grew older, I was allowed to go to midweek shows, especially if it was a good show and we had money. Any film would do, from westerns, romances and musicals, to the comedies.

When there were cowboys and Indians, or the United States cavalry and Indians, we all 'bagsed' being the good guys. Poor old Indians, they were left for dead: always the bad guys, especially the Apache and Comanche Nations. We whistled and yahooed when the cavalry came to the rescue of the palefaces to put down the Indians. I'm pretty sure that most of us grew up with the American notion that 'the only good Indian was a dead Indian' and started to believe it because of the way stories were told on the screen. We didn't know that they were only fighting for what was rightfully theirs, just as our own people are doing now.

I keep thinking how ignorant of the world we must have been, just going with the flow and copying the non-native kids in their vision of the Indian people. Sure, we felt sorry for the negro slaves in the Deep South and how they were mistreated and killed for nothing but felt differently towards the poor Red Indians. They were shown as being the savage murderers of the palefaces and the scum of the earth. Only in recent years are films made to show the Indian history of America, the lost Indian lifestyles and culture. While I was learning a little of Asian culture in Chinatown, I didn't know anything much about the African and American Indian cultures. Thank goodness I grew up and widened my horizons through reading and education.

All the same, I loved the picture shows and wondered why the full blood natives had to sit in the corral. I wanted to know why my little friends had to sit there, too. I kept asking my mimi why it was so. She must have got sick of my 'how come' questions whenever I went to the movies with her.

'How come you don't sit with Mimi Woey, hey? Or with Mimi Esther?'

'I told you about that before. You got no ears? You wanna go sit there? You go then. You'll see what's gonna happen to you when Mrs Anderson catch you. You ask too many questions, my girl!'

So I went to sit down with my mimis and little friends and learned that my Mimi Alice was right. I was taken by Mrs Anderson and shown to the front and was told not to go back there or I'd be sent outside. I was crying because I wanted to stay back there with my mimis and I couldn't.

Eventually, a number of years later, the little full blood kids were allowed to sit with us in the front rows. The corral took a bit longer to be dismantled so that the grown-ups could move freely amongst the other patrons. At one stage during the 1970s, I think, the theatre was closed and everyone thought that it was gone for

SUN PICTURES, 1950s

good. Somehow it re-opened in the 1980s but it didn't look the same or had the same atmosphere as in the days gone by.

On weekends or school holidays, when the town was almost deserted or in siesta time, the down-the-marsh kids played outside the Sun Pictures, acting out the scenes from past movies that we had seen.

'I bags being John Wayne.'

'No you can't. You're a girl.'

'Course I can. I don't have to be a boy.'

'I bags being Betty Grable.'

'You can't sing and dance. Ahha.'

''Course I can, just because you can't. You wanna see me?'

'I'll see you next year.'

'Well, you haven't got million dollar legs, anyway.'

'So? Who cares what kinda legs I got?'

The teasing and carrying on would go on until everyone settled down and then the action would begin. We'd strut around doing our acts and end up having a good time. On top of that, we had our own favourite film stars whom we picked out and 'owned'. No one was allowed to have the same ones because we'd be accused of copying them or robbing them but in our hearts we'd still love them and it would be our own secret, never telling anyone.

On picture show nights, we were all told to look out for each other when the show finished, especially when we were allowed to go out on our own. We were a bit older now and could go to the movies by ourselves. At the end of the show, we'd usually shake the sleeping kids and wait for them to get up even though Mrs Anderson would be hurrying us up because she was too impatient and wanted to close up as soon as possible. On several occasions though, we fell asleep ourselves and forgot to watch out for the other cousins. Sleepily, we walked outside with the crowd and waited for them to come out. We waited for a while and when there was no sign of them we all went home, thinking they had gone ahead of us.

'Where's Charlie, you two?' asked Aunty. 'The other kids came back, but not Charlie.'

She called out to Uncle and told him to go and look for Charlie. Aggie and I began to cry for him and Aunty gave us that 'what are you crying for' look. We went back with Uncle so that he could see what was the best way to get Charlie out of there. He told us to keep quiet and stay there while he headed home to get his big ladder. The house was only about a hundred yards away and he returned very shortly with the ladder and rope. He climbed over the wall and in about ten minutes we saw him come down the ladder with Charlie harnessed to him with the rope.

'Yay,' we cried, with tears rolling down our cheeks. 'How come you fell asleep, Charlie?'

He didn't answer us for he was still too sleepy to talk. We not only got a good growling from them that night but about twice more in the next few months, for we forgot Charlie again. We didn't mean to, we were only kids ourselves.

ROBINSON STREET

BY NOW WE WERE LIVING ON ROBINSON STREET, on a corner block with a big boab tree in the front yard and a poinciana and golden shower tree in the back. Around about Christmas, those trees were a spectacular sight, with their white, red and golden flowers in full bloom. It was in 1951 when we made that move. Circumstances had changed a little for the better; we seemed to have a few more clothes and shoes now, nothing terribly expensive but they were good enough for us. Even though we had a lot more food in the house, it didn't stop our mob from supplementing our food by way of fishing and hunting. Our mob still went short of money at times but it was a bit better than before.

It was a good move on my part, for the school was right across the road and I didn't have to walk those awful miles anymore. We still went to visit the down-the-marsh relatives nearly every day because it was one of the things we just did, whether it was from habit or because the family wanted to be in close contact daily. It was probably from the way of life our families always led, the togetherness of family living.

When I was a child only a few landowners such as the pearling masters and old lady Luna Rahman grew lots of mango trees. There were the odd one or two grown in people's yards and quite a number in the convent grounds as well. When Lulu Willy left Bungarun, he did odd jobs around the convent for the nuns and sometimes saved mangoes for us. The trees also provided shade all year round and about October and November their fruit were ready to be eaten. On our way to school or whenever we passed any mango trees, our mouths watered for them. We waited anxiously for the first of the ripened mangoes to fall and then we'd know that mango-eating time was on.

Mangoes were sold to anyone but sometimes we didn't have the sixpence or one shilling to buy them. Before and after school we'd run to Mrs McDaniel's to see if any mangoes fell outside the fence. Or, if the coast was clear, the big boys pulled down the overhanging branches and plucked the mangoes or they'd stone them down with shanghais. There'd be some mangoes just lying inside the fence and we'd look for big sticks to pull them towards us. Sometimes old Mr McDaniel shouted to us to get going otherwise he'd get his shotgun. We bolted all right! He never threatened to get the linju for us, only his shotgun.

We didn't know that we could pick up mangoes or any fruit that fell outside the fence.

Mimi Alice was working for Mrs McDaniel at that time and she'd bring mangoes home for us but we loved them so much that they were never enough for all of us. Whenever we called into Mrs McDaniel to see Mimi, we'd hope that she'd have saved some. If she didn't, she'd tell us to ask Mrs McDaniel, saying that the old lady wouldn't bite us.

I felt scared the first time I went to ask Mrs McDaniel for some mangoes. I knocked on the door and when I saw her coming I wanted to run away. Too late; I was frozen on the spot and when she'd asked what I wanted I could only gasp out, 'Have you got any old mangoes you don't want, please Missus?' My goodness, who in their right mind would ask for old mangoes!

'Yes, I have mangoes but you will have to sing me an Irish lullaby first.'

She knew that we were taught Irish songs and lullabies by the Irish nuns. She and Mr McDaniel were of Irish descent. I thought that only Tommy Tucker sang for his supper but here

I was singing for my mangoes. Anyway, I sang 'Danny Boy' and 'When Irish Eyes are Smiling' for her, any kind goes. She started to cry then went and got me some juicy mangoes, not old ones.

'That was really lovely, my dear. When you come again next time, I'd like you to sing "Danny Boy" for Mr McDaniel and me because we lost our own Danny Boy in the war, but we still love our Irish songs, no matter what.' I did just that the next time I went there. By then she knew that I was Alice's granddaughter.

She was a lovely old lady but nearly all of us were frightened of Mr McDaniel because we knew that he and old Freddy, his native houseboy, patrolled the grounds at night. They both wore white Wee Willy Winky gowns and carried a shotgun with them. We knew of the guns because we often saw them holding them, when going home after a basketball game or from the picture show, hoping we'd find some fallen mangoes on the way.

Sometimes we'd make plans during the week to go bushwalking at the back of the orphanage, on the common grounds. Our mums made sure that we took our younger sisters and cousins with us. They usually listened to us, so it wasn't too bad taking them along, I suppose. My boy cousins Jimmy and Alan Taylor, Billy Wright and Charlie, brought shanghais to shoot *jibalgru* for a feed, not shooting for sport. They were pretty good shooters and more times than not, caught quite a few jibalgru which were cooked for a feed when we got hungry. Sometimes we even brought some home for our mums, because they loved to eat them, too. While the boys hunted, my sister Barb, cousin Kitty Taylor, Aggie and I looked for *goongra, gubinge, magabala, njili njili*, moonga, *gum* or whatever bush fruit was in season. We always kept in touch by calling out to each other every now and again or by whistling in bird calls. Other kids did the same as we did and we often met up in the bush. When we got tired of looking for bush fruit we'd start playing hide'n'seek or chasey. Or we'd sit under the tree shade and tell stories. Sometimes we'd meet up with the orphanage girls for they often went bush walking with the Sisters and older girls.

We carried a water bag, bread and dripping sandwiches, some fruit and biscuits if they could be spared, just in case the boys caught nothing. The common grounds were very large in area and sometimes we wandered further away into the bush, often straying near or into the cemetery ground or near the ceremonial ground. That was definitely taboo, the ceremonial ground, so if we got nearer to it the boys made sure we backtracked away.

At the cemetery we were careful not to walk over unmarked graves or sunken ones, being ever so respectful for the lost ones and sort of superstitious at the same time, thanks to our mimis. We were told that if we ever stood on graves our feet would burn or other bad luck would follow us for the rest of our lives.

Well, one afternoon when we happened to stray into the cemetery, we met up with some orphanage girls and began visiting gravesites. Huge black clouds started gathering in the distance and it grew dark very quickly and Sister began clapping her hands to summon the girls to come back and get ready to go home. In Broome during cyclone season, it is quite common for late afternoon thunderstorms and heavy rain to develop suddenly, because of the tropical zone, I suppose. We could hear and smell the rain coming from miles away. As the rain came closer, the smell of it hitting the hot red sand, the black bitumen road surface and the dry grass just cannot be described. It's kind of euphoric. You either like or don't like it. Me? I just loved it.

I breathed in deeply to relish the smell while it lasted. It didn't last long enough for me though, because someone called out that it was getting darker and spookier, so we'd better head home. That warning cut short my breathing of the 'rainy fumes' and brought me back to my awareness of the cemetery which could look mighty scary at the best of times but in the dark no one had to give us a second warning to get moving. As we started running to beat the rain someone yelled, 'Yor yor! Jujud coming! Jujud coming!' That was it! We put on more speed and were off like lightning, stumbling and bumping into each other, tripping and falling into unmarked and sunken graves, praying like never before, blessing ourselves while on the run.

'Please God. Please God. Save my feet. Save my feet. I don't want burnt feet.'

I prayed silently in my mind, at the same time imagining myself running on two burnt black stumps at the end of two skinny legs. I wasn't a very fast runner but kept up with the rest of the girls, I assure you. I don't think we stopped running until we reached Luna Rahman's place. All of us had stitches in our sides, some of us bending over to stop the pain while the rest of us were lying on the ground under a tree, catching our breath. Naturally, we all laughed about it afterwards, teasing each other about who was the most scared one and who took off first. We looked like drowned rats when we finally reached home.

Living in Robinson Street also meant that it was further for us to walk to Chinatown to see the picture shows, or movies, as it was becoming popularly known. On Saturday nights if our parents weren't at home, we'd get dressed and make our way to

Mr Dep's gambling house to see if they had picture money for us. On the way there we'd be in very high spirits, talking about the movie that was screening that night. Children weren't allowed in the gaming dens so we usually looked through the windows or around the room to see whether the linju were around. If the coast was clear, we'd make a dash to the tables and ask for picture money. Most times we were lucky because they had money for us, after having a win.

Other times we had to walk all the way back home, the high spirits having left us. No more laughing and joking, no more getting excited to see our friends there, just blaming ourselves for being stupid enough to go there for nothing. That didn't deter us though, for we'd do it again the following Saturday if our parents weren't home. All this didn't mean that our parents didn't go to the movies with us on a Saturday night; they usually did, especially if it was a good movie.

Sometimes when they had no money, they'd feel sorry for us and would tell us to wait at Aunty's house or outside old Anawai's shop in case they had a win in the meantime. Or there might be some aunty or uncle there to shout us in. There were two shows every picture night, the feature being shown last, but we didn't care if missed the first one, for we'd usually find a crack in the sheet iron wall and take turns peeping at the movie. They'd tell us that if we didn't see them by 'endable' time or interval time (when we eventually worked out what 'endable' meant), we were to start walking back home.

Whenever we walked to the movies, we had to pass the old courthouse which looked very spooky in the darkness. The street lighting wasn't too well lit and we'd avoid looking in that direction. Several times in the ensuing years, we swore that we saw a figure of a man dangling from the rafters above the verandah, with a rope around his neck. Everyone said that we imagined it but we stuck to our story. We saw it; they didn't.

Broome is full of ghost stories and scary places, anyway and I'm sure that those stories are still doing their rounds, with newer ones to boot. We were also told that devils lived in the cork trees and came out at night for children and that if we were to dig up the trees, we'd find dead people's bones under them. I could well believe that, for they are the ugliest looking trees, gaunt and gnarled and have the vilest of smell, ever.

The first time we ever played near cork trees was when we saw their 'flowers' falling from their branches. They looked like tiny helicopters twirling downwards to land and we were fascinated by them. As we ran to pick them up we just had to comment on the trees ugly appearance. Trees couldn't have those things as 'flowers,' could they? Then of course, we just had to smell them and they were so foul. We poked a small hole into the tree and watched the slimy juice ooze out. Aggie and I just had to touch it and smell it, too. Well, it was so vile and overpowering that it knocked the wind out of us and we staggered around like drunken bulls for what seemed like hours. After that we really believed those stories our mob told us. At night the trees looked very spooky and their branches looked as if they were going to reach out and grab us. We sure avoided walking the streets or back roads that had cork trees growing there. I don't even know if they are native to Australia. If they aren't, then whoever brought them here must have come from an ugly country. I don't think that I've ever seen them outside Broome country, although I did hear that some were found growing outside Port Hedland on one of the stations.

It was Easter weekend of 1954, after the basketball games were played and we were all in high spirits going home. There were Pearly and Sally, Eileen, Philip and Dominic Matsumoto, their mum and of course, me walking back home as we all lived around Robinson Street, so it was natural for us to walk home together. I think Julie and Pauline Mamid and Doris were there as well. Just as we were nearing McDaniel's corner, we heard screams from the gaol house or up the hill area. We took no notice of the screaming, saying that they were just kids mucking around. It did sound terrifying, though and sent cold shivers down our spines. By the time we reached that corner, the two boys and their mum were way ahead of us. I don't know whether or not they heard the screams the first time around. Pearly was on a bike, pedalling slowly, because the rest of us were walking at a normal pace and we were all laughing and talking at the same time, not really caring what was going on around us.

As we walked and talked, one of the girls said, 'Hey, you guys! Listen! Can you still hear the screaming? It sounds like it's coming from the Post Office now.'

So we all stopped to listen. Sure enough, there were screams coming from that direction but we still took no notice of them, saying they must be the Indian Territory kids fooling around. We still carried on laughing and talking until we passed McDaniel's corner. The screams were getting closer and closer now. Soon there were the sounds of running feet, thumping the sandy ground and then the terrified sounds of a woman's cries for help.

'Help me! Wait for me! Help me!' she called out from behind us, the voice now coming directly from the Post Office area, which was almost in total darkness.

'Yor yor!' we screamed in unison. Well, that was all we needed (as usual). We started to run with fright ourselves, not knowing who or what was behind us. Tul-tul-tul went our own feet on the bitumen! Pearly was still on her bike but couldn't keep up with us. We all had the same thoughts in our heads, whoever was chasing that woman might grab us too, or sling us to the ground and kill us. We weren't going to wait and find out! Finally, we reached my house on the corner, huffing and puffing, pulling up winded. Luckily there was street lighting on that corner. So we waited for that woman to emerge from the darkness. She was in a collapsed state, exhausted from the running and the fright she must have had. As she drew nearer to the light, we could see the terror on her face and soon recognised her.

'It's Mary Drummond,' said Pearly. 'What's happened, Mary?'

She was bent over and trying to catch her breath and talk to us at the same time.

'How come you guys never stopped for me? You guys must have heard me screaming and yelling my guts out?'

'We heard you but we thought it was some kids mucking around, true God. We got frightened ourselves and we just took off, too. It was horrible to hear the screams,' replied Pearly.

Mary told us that she was playing cards in Indian Territory and that she usually went home to One Mile in a taxi. That night she had changed her mind and decided to walk to her sister Irene Torres' place to sleep over till morning. She took a short cut near the gaol house where the big, old tamarind tree stood. That tamarind tree was every kid's stopping place after school. It was big and shady, had the sweetest fruit when ripe and was a mighty tree to climb and to play Tarzan games.

Anyway, as she neared the tree, she saw a normal-sized black dog standing there, softly growling at her. When she got closer, it suddenly grew larger in size, its eyes were glowing into a fiery red colour and looked as if it had a fiery tongue as well. It was starting to move towards her, circling around her and snarling at her every time it came around to face her. Her hands and arms felt frozen and she couldn't move. In a short while her fingers began to move and she slowly reached for her cigarettes and matches, moving it upwards towards her mouth. When it circled and snarled again, she quickly struck the match and flicked it on the dog. In seconds it disappeared right in front of her and that was the chance she needed to cut for it. When she got near the Post Office, she heard it coming behind her, growling and snarling more ferociously than ever so she just ran and ran, screaming with fright, not looking back until she caught up to us under the light. After telling us her story and catching her breath again, she took off like lightning, never stopping until she reached Irene's place.

A couple of days later, she told Pearly and Sally that when she reached Irene's house, she told her sister all about it and they shut all the doors and windows and went to bed. Mary said that she had slept like a log until morning but poor Irene couldn't go to sleep at all, just shaking with fright thinking that the dog might

OLD BROOME POST OFFICE, 1958

still be outside waiting for them because they heard something walking around and around the house.

There were many stories about that big black dog, long before that incident with Mary and there'll be more to come. After being a near witness, I'll always believe Mary's story and will never forget it.

I'm pretty certain that almost every child growing up in Broome would have heard the 'Red Dress Woman' and the 'Handsome Man with Bullock Feet' stories of those frightening times. The woman in red appeared out of nowhere, usually after midnight. Car drivers ran into her and when they'd look back to see, she'd still be standing there looking back at them. Men and women saw her but no one ever stopped to check her out. Too frightened, I guess. My Uncle Tommy Taylor told us that he often saw her walking near the old Native Hospital when he worked the graveyard shift at the powerhouse. After a while he'd just say to Aunty Peggy, 'Hey, Peggo, I saw that red dress woman again.'

That 'handsome man' lured the young native women to drink in the bush outside town. He'd hang around the pub near his car and chat up the girls inviting them to drink with him.

'Why not,' they asked each other. 'We'll drink his gurry anytime. We won't knock back his gurry.'

The big bottles of Emu Bitter seemed endless, never running out. As the women got drunker, more bottles seemed to be replaced like magic. They didn't mind; they didn't have to buy the bottles. Later on, one of the women began to wonder why he wasn't drunk like they were, at the same time looking at him, giving him the once over, until her eyes stopped and looked at his feet. Funny kind of shoes he was wearing, she thought, looked more like bullock feet. She then gave her friend a sign to go behind the bushes for goomboo. She whispered in lingo to her.

'Yow jidja. El-double-oh. El-double-oh-tee. Must be *ngeera*. Let's gee-oh, never mind we're pieces.'

The other woman didn't wait to look. She believed her friend and in seconds flat they were off, running all the way into town. When they reached home, they were as sober as two old judges.

There were many other similar stories to this at different times over the years and the women still swear that his feet were cloven. That same 'handsome devil' also played cards with the local gamblers and for weeks the old gamblers talked about the uncanny luck of the stranger. He just couldn't go wrong, scooping them just about every night, as some old timers said that he'd gamble with them, losing at first but winning them all at the end. They said he must have *djirri*; his luck was faultless. He learned all the different games that the people played, even the Chinese games of kaja-kaja in which domino-like slabs were used.

It probably would have gone on forever but for one night when a player happened to drop a kaja-kaja stick (slab) on the floor. When he bent to pick it up, he saw a pair of cloven feet sticking out of the stranger's trouser legs. Well, if a black man could turn white with fright it probably happened that night. He just sat there shaking, figuring how he could tell the others without drawing the stranger's attention to himself. After the stranger scooped them once again, he left the room and the gamblers high and dry, as usual. It was then that the story of the cloven feet was told to the gamblers.

'I knew there was something about that man.'

'I told you he must have djirri. He was too good for us.'

'Waddow. To think I was sitting right next to him. Waddow. Gives me the cold shivers.'

'Well there now, you guys. More you want to play with handsome guys.'

After that story got around, the gambling stranger disappeared but he still appeared to native girls every now and again.

One of the many private gambling houses belonged to old lady Esther Corpus. It was in the vicinity of Robinson Street and behind Uncle Henry D'Antoine's place, within walking distance of most players, Mum's especially. My mum, Aunty Kudjie and Aunty Mary Cox went there one afternoon and naturally, their kids went with them. The yard was fairly large and had several big, shady trees that were meant for climbing. It was a bit sprinkly that day, with signs of heavy rain coming our way, probably during the night. It wasn't too wet that we couldn't play outdoors, so we started to play the usual games of hide'n'seek and drop the hanky, as there were plenty of kids outside waiting to play. We had been warned not to climb the trees because the branches would be too slippery and dangerous.

'You guys better not go climbing the trees, you hear? You might fall down and crack your head,' warned our mums, their voices meaning business.

Tracey Cox and I were just standing around talking to several other kids under the tallest of the trees, which happened to be a very good climbing tree, trying to figure out what game we should play first. Of course, some kids were already up in the tree, swinging from branch to branch, taking no notice of their mums. Aggie was one of them.

'Look! Look!' she cried. 'I can climb the highest! I can beat anyone! Haw-haw! Only me!'

'You better come down, Aggie. You know what Aunty said,' shouted Tracey and me. 'You're just skiting. Just come down!'

'I won't fall down,' she replied, climbing even higher. Our shouting must have made her feel game. It fell on deaf ears.

The kids were still mucking about on the tree for another ten minutes or so when we heard the 'kerrack-kerrack' of a branch trying desperately to crack. Next minute we heard the final 'kerrack' immediately followed by a terrifying scream and the thud-thud-thud of a small body hitting just about every other branch on the way down. The little body made a final thud about a yard away from us. It was Aggie. She was knocked clean out of breath and lay motionless on her side in a crumbled heap. It happened so fast that we couldn't do anything to help her. I went running and crying inside to tell Aunty and Mum about the accident. By the time they came out, Aggie was sitting up holding her arm, pointing to her elbow, which was jutting out almost to her upper arm. While Aunty was gathering her up in her arms and getting ready to go to the hospital, my Mum was shaking me and giving me a few whacks on my legs with a skinny stick.

'You should've been keeping an eye on them kids. You guys were told not to go climbing up trees in this weather. Look what happened now. You can't listen to us?' Mum said to all of us.

'But I did listen. I didn't climb trees. Those other kids did. You can ask Tracey.'

'Never mind about that. You're the oldest here and you should've been watching those kids.'

'Yeah but they don't listen to us big kids, anyway.'

I couldn't win an argument so I stayed quiet as Mum and I followed Aunty and Aggie to the hospital. Luckily it was only around the corner. Aggie was found to have a dislocated elbow, so mother and daughter were sent to Perth the next day. She had her operation on the 5th of August 1954 but Aggie spent almost four months down there at Lady Lawley's Cottage to recuperate.

It turned out to be a complicated dislocation, with her sinews being severed and so on. It was a successful operation the doctors said but her arm and elbow had to be pinned together forever but her arm was never the same, up to this very day. Aggie never ever blamed us for her fall from that tree because she knew she was told not to climb it and was only showing off for us.

Further down the Robinson Street area lived Mr Horry Miller and his family. He was one of the founders of MacRobertson Miller Airlines and married to Mary Durack, the author who was from the pioneering stock of the Durack family in the Kimberley and who later became Dame Mary Durack. She came to the school on a few occasions to give talks to us about writing books and art. She and her sister Elizabeth were accomplished artists in their chosen fields and we felt honoured because they were Kimberley people who were connected to Aboriginal people on the station. Mr Miller often took boys and girls for sky rides in his plane and they all loved it. He didn't care who the kids were as they all behaved themselves and enjoyed the rides. Whenever kids saw him, with his unmistakable white hair blowing in the wind, they'd all yell out his name, 'Mr Miller, Mr Miller!' and he'd wave back with his familiar gesture. I think that later on the family used to come back on school holidays because they lived in Perth. We'd see them at Mass on Sundays.

Our house was very large and was a shared accommodation with a common kitchen and separate living areas, enclosed by large verandahs which were partly latticed. There were storm-shutters right around the verandahs and they were propped up with wooden poles to let in the cool breeze. During cyclones the shutters were bolted from the insides for protection from the fierce winds and rain. There were a few cyclones hitting the town or nearby coast during my childhood. Some were scary but people weathered the storm all right. It was after the cyclone that was the best time. Kids were out in the streets or in town looking for coins that were unearthed. It's surprising how many coins were found for us to spend.

Our house was shared with Aunty Susie Dolby and her family. Sometimes both Mum and Aunty Susie ran cards there. One day when they were playing cards, Granny May Howard happened to go broke first and was out of the game, so Aunty Susie asked her to sit on the verandah and keep watch for the linju.

'If you see linju coming, you gotta cough to signal us, okay? We'll give you another start to play again after,' Aunty told her.

Only a few of the players knew about Granny May and the arrangement. Mum and Aunty Susie took it for granted that if they were raided and made a run for the doors, the others would know and follow suit. They simply forgot to mention it, especially when they were all enjoying themselves, laughing and joking as they usually do, time slipping away and poor Granny May forgotten by everyone. After a couple of hours playing cards and greatly enjoying themselves and deeply engrossed in the game, they were suddenly alerted by the sounds of someone clearing his throat, followed by a coughing spasm.

The 'select few' looked at each other and someone called out, 'Linju! Linju! Let's gee-oh!' In their haste, the 'select few' knocked their chairs over, knocked over some onlookers and rushed out the back through the kitchen door and went flying into the little outhouse. The others were left stunned in their seats, wondering what on earth was going on.

Anyway, the group of six, including a man, had crammed into

the little outhouse, covering their noses and trying to keep quiet. They were sweating profusely and jammed up against each other like sardines. After about twenty minutes they decided that the linju must have left. Back they went, cautiously peeping around the door of the kitchen before going to the players' room.

'Them linju went away?'

'What linju? No linju here. Where have you guys been, anyway? You left us for dead. We're still waiting for the cards to be dealt.'

'You never heard that coughing? That was the warning signal for Jidja May to give us for the linju. Where is she, anyway?'

'May's not here. Last time we saw her she was getting a jug of water and went outside. She never told us anything about signals. You guys mean to say that you left us here for the linju to catch us playing? You guys got no shame to do that to us.'

'We thought you guys would know when we took off. We wouldn't scatter for nothing.'

'Yow. Wadda gee, girl,' exclaimed Aunty Susie, suddenly remembering Granny May. 'Jidja May must be still outside.'

When they went to check her out, sure enough, she was still sitting in the same place.

'Jidja May, where that linju?'

'What linju? Linju never come. Who said linju was here?'

'Well, what were you coughing for then?'

'That was me coughing because my throat was getting itchy and I couldn't stop coughing. It was too itchy so I went to get water and forgot all about the coughing signal until I saw you guys rushing out the back. That other mob didn't know what was going on and I didn't tell them anything, too.'

Everyone just looked at each other and burst out laughing. They went back inside to recap on the whole incident and laughed the night away. Whenever any new player came along, they had to tell the story again and again.

There were many good times in that house on Robinson Street, what with Aunty Susie and Aunty Vera Dann and Mum sharing the big old house. Aunty Vera moved in when she left the convent life. Those two aunties used to fill the house with songs, stories and laughter especially with stories about Beagle Bay.

SIBLINGS

THIS IS ONE STORY THAT UNCLE JACOB told us about my little sister Barbara. My mum worked at the District Hospital and either my mimis or Aunty Kudjie had to help look after her. I was still at the orphanage so it was only Barb that had to be minded. My other aunties worked as housemaids until they got married themselves. Any child minding was shared by the families whenever the mums had outside work to do.

One particular day was different. Mum had to go to work and Aunty had to take Aggie and Charlie somewhere. Guess who had to look after Barb? Uncle Jacob, of course. He wasn't working at the time so he was stuck with the job of babysitting.

'You're not doing anything Jacob, so you watch Barbara for today. I have to go somewhere and Aggie has to work. You can get Jularu to help you if you want. Aggie should be home about four o'clock. I might be back early but I don't know for sure.'

Uncle really wanted to go and play cards that day so he went to look for Jularu but he was nowhere to be found. It must have been his lucky day, for who should turn up to visit was none other that Mr and Mrs Chi, a Chinese couple who had no children and were friends of Uncle and Aunty. Uncle asked them to mind Barb for a little while and they were quite willing to care for her.

'More better me buy Buballa.'

'I no can do, Missus. She belong Aggie. I no can sell Barbara.'

'Buballa good baby. We take her to China. You sell me Buballa, yes?'

Uncle was anxious to play a few hands before the two sisters got back, so still arguing with the Chi's about Barbara, he left her with the couple shaking his head with a big 'no' to them.

Around three o'clock he looked at his watch and hurried home. No Barb! No Mr and Mrs Chi! All sorts of things went through his mind. Aggie and Kudjie will be home soon. Thank goodness they're not back yet. I better go and look for Barbara and the two Chinamen.

When he reached the Chi's place he found them at home and went to pick up Barb but Mrs Chi tried to stop him. The biggest argument developed between Uncle and the Missus with Barb caught in a tug-of-war, being pulled this way and that way. While they were tugging away, old man Chi was trying to put some money in Uncle's shirt pocket.

'You say Buballa mine! I give you plenty money. You take money. I take Buballa.'

'No, no! Barbara belong Aggie. Must take Barbara back. Bumbye Aggie and Kudjie give me good hiding.'

'You say Buballa mine! I take to China. Here money. I buy.'

'Aggie and Kudjie come back soon. Bumbye sergeant and policeman come for Barbara. Bumbye they report you and you go gaol.'

Barb changed hands several times between the two Chinamen with Uncle dancing with each of them and baby in the middle. Old Missus grabbed Barb and rushed into a room, closely followed by Uncle who in turn was followed by the old man. They must have been arguing and waltzing around with Barb, running in and out of the rooms, for about half an hour, so eventually and quite reluctantly they handed her back to Uncle.

He just made it back home as the two sisters pulled up in a taxi. Luckily for him, otherwise there'd be a bigger row than he had with the Chi's. He didn't tell them about it until much, much later when they were all in a jovial mood,. Mr and Mrs Chi still remained friends with them even though they still humbugged Mum for their Buballa.

Sadly, they eventually went back to China without their Buballa.

In May of 1951, when I was nine years old, my baby brother Alexanda was born and my life took on another change. I now had a few more responsibilities but did not realise how many until it was put into practice. My baby brother was a delight to us, being the firstborn boy in the family and also a new baby brother for Barb and me. Sure, Aggie and I used to help bath our baby sister, brothers and cousins, change their nappies and powder them up but with my very own new baby brother it was somehow different. So at an early age, we were taught to care and mind our own little ones. My second baby brother Henry joined our family about a year later and it became an even more hectic household, especially with Mum now getting asthma attacks more often. Helping out was expected of us and that was that, so we all grew up with those teachings from our mothers.

I did learn useful things at home other than getting up to mischief and the silliness of my youth. Mum taught me how to cook and sew, to wash my clothes by hand and iron them properly, not quick goes. On washing days, either my aunties or other mimis came over to help us do the laundry. It kind of reminded me of the mission on laundry days. Sometimes it wasn't possible to get anyone to help and we did it on our own. I didn't do the heavy washing until I was about eleven or twelve but it was no big deal because I wasn't a sickly child and quite strong. We didn't have a washing machine and when Mum had her sick days, I had to wash and scrub the sheets, pillow slips and towels with a scrubbing brush and washing board, then boil the clothes in a large copper. Sometimes she did get a washerwoman named Lena when she was in town and not out bush with her husband. Because I was so short, it was a real headache for me to hang up the clothes. I had to stand on a wooden fruit box and drag it along the clothesline that was propped up with a long, forked tree branch.

There was also a wood stove in the house which meant that wood had to be chopped and stacked. I don't know how many times I smoked out the house and people until I got the hang of lighting it properly: no one had told me about the flue.

You may wonder why we'd go to town to see if our parents had picture money or why they weren't home for other reasons. That didn't mean we were neglected or that we had no food in the house. It meant that lunch or dinner was already cooked and left for us to heat up or there was food in the fridge (by then we had an electric fridge) and we could cook whatever we fancied because, my mum especially, knew that I could cook and would feed the others. I think that as I grew older and approached adolescence, the mature part of me balanced out the stupid things of my childhood. We just had to look out for each other.

The appearance of Alex in my life kind of meant that now I had another child to look after, as if Barb wasn't enough. I had my grumble times as much as anyone else and at times I resented it when I wasn't allowed to go and play with my friends. It was okay when it was only Barb and me because she had the other cousins and friends to play with, even though they hung around and followed us almost everywhere, anyway. This was different; babies can't hang around with big kids, surely?

Alex was indeed a beautiful baby, if you can call boy babies beautiful. He had lots of black hair and his most noticeable feature was his ever so long eyelashes, which were so thick and long that they curled up and almost touched his eyebrows. He walked at eight months and talked in sentences before he was one year old. I remember quite well the day he walked. Mum was in the kitchen and I was reading a comic on the floor, at the same time watching over him. He was crawling about and all of a sudden he just stood up, hands free, and walked towards me. I was shocked and called out to Mum to come and see him but he fell down. That didn't stop him and he was up again, walking towards Mum's direction in a running motion. I couldn't believe it because most babies crawl and try to pull themselves up by way of a chair or table leg and slowly take a few steps at a time. Not Alex; he just flew on his little feet, never stopping until he'd tire and sit down. During all this time, Alex was the apple of our eyes, with Barb being the littlest mother to him, feeding him with the bottle and pushing him around the house in the big, cream-coloured cane pram.

It was a little over a year later that my other brother Henry joined the family. His black hair was also long and thick, reaching almost to his little shoulders. His eyelashes weren't as long as Alex's but he was a beautiful baby. Now there were two babies to push around in the pram, up and down Robinson Street.

They were a handful! I was ten years old and had two baby boys to mind. I loved my baby brothers but they were a drag and I didn't want to mind them all weekend. I wanted to go and play with my friends. If Mum was sick, then that was different; we had to help. There were times when Barb and I thought that they were unreasonable demands on us but we did them anyway.

At about twelve years of age, I began to notice that the older girls had smooth, shiny legs and girls in my age group began copying them by shaving their legs as well. They told me that it was easy to do and didn't I want my legs to look like the Hollywood stars?

Hairy legs looked too mannish, they said. All the movie stars shaved their legs, they said. Well, they said all kinds of things to us twelve year olds and they sounded better and better every time they opened their mouths. So guess what Miss Copy Cat did? Yes, she did it. I now had smooth legs like the movie stars. Two weeks later, the hairs came back in double length size! Nobody told us that this would happen. Nobody told us that we'd have gorilla-like legs for the rest of our lives unless we continually shaved and shaved. They grew so long that I was sure that I could easily plait them. A fair price to pay for vanity in our youth, I suppose.

Once, when Mum went to town, I got out her dressmaking scissors and trimmed Alex's eyelashes. I was thinking that since the hairs on my legs grew longer after shaving, surely the eyelashes on Alex would grow longer and lush. I wouldn't tell Mum and I'd surprise her with Alex's new eyelashes. My dreams were short lived. Two days later, I could hear her shouting at Dad.

'Ala! Ala! Come here! Look at this boy. Look at his eyes. Just look. Did you cut his eyelashes? Come on, tell me. You're the only one with hair cutting gear. It must have been you.'

ALA AND ALEX, BROOME

190

'What, Aggie? You think I'm *munjung*? I'm not that silly. Ask them kids.'

'Don't blame the kids,' she said, beckoning to Barb and me at the same time. 'Do you know who done this? Did you see anyone do this thing?'

We both stayed silent for a long time. Mum was the only one going off her head, still arguing with Dad. Finally, after about ten minutes silence, I told her that I had done it. I made sure that I was standing a long way from her.

'What? You could have blinded your brother. Who told you that you could cut his eyelashes? Twelve years old and you still do stupid things.'

'No one did. I only wanted his eyelashes to grow longer. I didn't mean to do it.'

'Well, don't you dare touch those eyelashes again? Or Henry's, you hear?'

I could only nod for the hundredth time, it seemed. I hadn't thought that I could be harming Alex's eyes and eyesight. I only wanted him to have beautiful, long lashes, because I certainly didn't have any.

Whenever my friends made plans to meet up somewhere or whenever I wanted to go to the shops, I had to ask Mum first.

'Yeah, you can go but take Alex and Henry with you.'

'But I'm only going to Ellies Store. I'll be back straight away.'

'Just take Alex and Henry and use the pram.'

Most times I'd forget about it but if I was really desperate to go, I'd take them with me. Maybe it was Mum's way of keeping me at home. I don't know, but my brothers, Barb, the cane pram and I were a regular sight to see on Robinson Street.

We also had a pet billy goat named Patsy. Someone gave it to

Dad and he brought it home thinking it was a nanny goat so that we could have fresh goat's milk whenever we wanted it, because Mum knew how to milk goats. When Mum told him that it was a billy goat and shouldn't be called Patsy, Dad just shrugged his shoulders and said it was okay to call it Patsy because Patsy didn't know a boy's name from a girl's name. That made sense.

Anyway, Patsy became a dear pet to us. He followed us everywhere, from home to school, to the shops in town, to the pictures at night and even to Mass on Sundays. To stop him from following us, we tried to tie him up with a rope but somehow he'd get loose so we were stuck with him. When people in town saw Patsy, they'd know that one of us was near.

'Patsy's coming. It must be Ala or Aggie coming along.'

We just could not get away from Patsy. He'd even follow us to the beach, keeping a short distance from us. He never came onto the beach, though. He just happily helped himself to the grass and shrubs growing around there. Others thought that it was great to have a pet goat around the place and it was, but it was a nuisance too. We kept Patsy for another year or so before he died. On Robinson Street it just wasn't the same without Patsy and everybody sure missed him.

SCHOOL DAYS

AT SCHOOL IN BROOME

IN BROOME THERE WERE TWO SCHOOLS, the state school, Broome Primary School, and the convent school, St Mary's Primary School. We called them the state school kids and goodness knows what else they called us besides 'Catholic dogs stink like frogs.' The two schools were 'mortal enemies' and there were a few fights going on, boy or girls, especially in the first few weeks of each new school year. There were usually new kids in both schools so they had to test themselves out.

After the fights died down all was quiet until someone started it up again. There were also fights going on between kids in their own schools as well. The whole school knew when there was a fight going on, whether it was between the state school versus the convent or just boy versus boy or girl versus girl, because the news spread like wildfire. After school the 'outside' kids made a beeline to the decided venue, where the fight was going to take place. The spectators had 'bagsed' their places for a better view. Then it was on! Kids barracked loudly for their mates, shouting abuse to each other and forming a huge circle around the boxers. They followed the moving circle round and round, back and forth, this way and that way. It was a sight to see! Sometimes other small fights broke out from that one, boys promising themselves with 'Me and you next time, boy' and 'Yeah mate, I'll catch you tomorrow' and 'You wait. I'll fly you.'

If it wasn't the linju breaking them up, it was mums and dads or passersby who tried. Usually it was the little brothers or sisters who blew the whistle to their parents. Poor little souls would be branded with 'tell-tale-tit' or 'blabber-mouth' for days on end.

I don't know what exactly made the boys fight each other. It was probably bullying or thinking they were better than each other, like being the best athlete or boxer or maybe it was the smart-alecky talk amongst them that started most fights.

The state school kids were mostly white kids or native kids who were being brought up as whites or Asians, because their fathers were of either race. Most of us were half-caste kids anyway but our mob identified ourselves as natives or 'Aboriginals', as it was now becoming fashionable for natives to be described. We just naturally followed our mother's side of the family line as there were more Aboriginals in our family line than there were whites or Asians.

There was no real law to say how you should raise your children or which school your child should attend, just the one about natives not being allowed into state schools unless it was approved by the rest of the white parents, or something like that. They probably got accepted on their father's merits anyway. Or perhaps it was a religious issue, as some natives may not have been Catholic.

It is a pity about those children though. Some of them were originally attending the convent school but later on the trend was for kids to go to the state school. Perhaps the worst fear for the parents was that St Mary's was an Aboriginal school or 'binghi' school as it was referred to by some of the uppity, coloured Broome community.

Some of those children probably never knew their people, never sat on the ground with their mimis telling them stories, never being taken to *kubba kubbas* and other ceremonies, never spoke in broken English and probably never spoken to a full blood adult person let alone their full blood children.

What a loss! Those children were denied their Aboriginal heritage and knowledge, the things that most of us take for granted, the things that must have been as embarrassment to the 'better blacks' of the time. That was how it was in those days, I suppose. Some wore their heritage with pride, others hid theirs.

Perhaps there may be a hint of subtle bitterness in this part of my story and maybe it's a carry over from when the Beagle Bay and Lombadina people weren't really accepted by their own native townspeople. I heard my Mum and other mission women talking about how town natives, or 'better blacks', made hurtful remarks about them when they were new to town life. They were called the 'mission natives,' 'barefoot natives who don't know how to wear shoes or boots', 'those mission people who can't even speak proper English' and 'they don't know how to live in houses.' Some of the really old women were laughed at when they wore another skirt under their dresses.

'Don't they know how to wear petticoats under their dresses, instead of another coloured, cotton skirt?'

They thought themselves too good for our mission people, I suppose. Around about that time, Broome may have been getting too overcrowded with mission people and it was time for some to move to other places, Darwin or Perth or even interstate to larger cities, where native people knew how to live, speak and dress better.

It is amazing how the overall recognition of Aboriginals as people in their own rights, the Land Rights Movement, the Native Title Act, the Stolen Generation, Aboriginal languages, Aboriginal Deaths in Custody and other Aboriginal issues have brought back many of those people to 're-settle in their proper country' and in Broome town.

It makes me want to weep for my grandparents, Mum and family people, but who wants to be eternally morbid in this short life on earth? My mum would have wanted me to get on with life and move forward.

ST MARY'S STUDENTS WITH BISHOP RAIBLE AND VISITING CLERGY, c1956

Going to a Catholic school also meant that we had to prepare ourselves for the next stage of the Seven Sacraments, since we already used up the first one: Baptism. Since kindergarten we were taught the catechism in dribs and drabs (because we were littlies) but the importance of our religious beliefs were instilled in us at that tender age. By the time we were in Class 3 we were fully instructed and prepared to receive the Sacraments of Confession and Holy Communion. We knew the Ten Commandments, the Seven Sacraments and the Cardinal Sins off by heart, not parrot fashion but fully understanding them. We were proud of that.

I was still living down the marsh and as time was drawing nearer, I was getting a bit excited at the thought of my big day and the Breakfast. Mum had made me a white dress and veil and had splurged out on a new pair of white sandals and sovks. I was dying to have a new pair of white patent shoes with buckles and bows but they were out of our reach. They looked so beautiful sitting on the shelf in Kennedy's Store. Anyway, I was just happy to have new white footwear, not white sandshoes, for a change.

We went to Mass almost every Sunday but the big day worried me. What if I were to sleep in and miss it? All kinds of thoughts went through my little mind in the days leading up to it. Mum kept assuring me that we'd all go on time but I was still nervous at the thought of missing my big day. So Aggie and I had a little plan in mind. Mum had all my clothes ready in the room and on the Saturday night before, we gathered all my clothes in a neat bundle and walked to the courthouse building to hide them, even though we were scared of the place. Every shadow made us flinch inside and the deeper we went under the building the more frightened we became but the thought of missing my big day was greater so we hastily hid the clothes and went back to town to wait for the picture show to start.

At four o'clock in the morning, I woke Aggie and we went outside to shower up and wait for the sun to rise. I was fasting since midnight and dying to have a drink but no way was I going to break it. It was harder in those days, about fasting I mean. So we sat on the front steps and when we thought it was time to go, we started walking to the courthouse to dress. We knew it was too early for Mass so we lingered around the courthouse until we saw churchgoers making their way to the church and we followed suit.

While everybody started to get ready to go inside the church and as we communicants had a last minute look at ourselves, tidying our veils and dresses, my family came rushing into the churchyard and headed straight for me. Aggie was already seated as she wasn't one of the communicants; she was my little helper.

'Why didn't you wait for us? You know we wouldn't let you down and where's Aggie, anyway?' asked Mum looking around for her *goombali*.

'We went looking everywhere in Chinatown for you two.

You had us worried. Lucky Uncle said we better check the church anyway, just in case you went there early part,' said Aunty Kudjie.

'I'm sorry but I had to make sure for myself. I had to get here early.' I was glad that they made it for my big day and after Mass they joined us for the big Breakfast. I knew that Mum understood and later when we went home, she reassured me once again.

In every school year there were seasons which rotated almost like nature's own cycle. There were marble season, knucklebone season, skipping rope season and 'lecky band' season, to name a few. Someone would bring in marbles to play and before you knew it, everyone would be playing, little kids and big kids, girls and boys. The playground was full small groups playing for 'keeps' or for 'funs'. Girls who didn't have marbles would beg or ask, 'I can play fun-go? I can play fun-go, jidja?'

Of course, the playground was divided into boys and girls areas, so that there was no mixing of the sexes then, which had its own merits, for I'd rather get a slap in the face from a girl than a punch in the mouth by a boy. There were a few times when boy and girl did mix it, though, with the kids yelling out, 'Hand go. Hand go,' to alert all the others and to bring Sister, for she had the job of breaking up the fight. So thank goodness we had our own side.

One time ago there was a boy–girl fight starting in the church and spilling onto the grounds outside. It was hit for hit and poor old Father McKelson was caught in the middle, trying to break them up. It was just awful, starting up from a love note found in the boy's desk and the boy took offence. Everyday, the girls went out first but that day Father said the boys could go out first and that was that. It was the chance the boy was waiting for and caught the girl coming down the steps. We were screaming with fright as Father tried to break up the pair. Thank goodness he did.

After school the 'outside' kids walked home together going in different directions and playing 'following taw'. They usually ended up playing 'big ring' or 'poison hole' in front of someone's home. The usual bickering went on when someone cheated or won all the marbles. It was the crack shots who kept winning and who were accused of cheating in every game, which wasn't the case at all. It was their excellent skills and no one was credited with those skills even though they were very good shooters. I wasn't very good at playing marbles but enjoyed playing the different games. As we girls began growing up, interest in the games began to wane. Besides, our bigger skirts became too cumbersome for us to play properly and we had to bunch up the front of the skirt and tuck it between our knees, making it awkward for us to hunch over for a good shot. Also, we didn't want our *jowidge* showing.

Another reason for my losing interest was the forming of groups. Now that the games were becoming more competitive, kids were going around asking, 'You be my company?' or 'You and me go company with Mary, hey?' If you had a run-in with your partner, straight away she'd say, 'Gimme back my marbles, then. I'm gonna go company with someone else. So there.' By the end of season I ended up with no marbles and no company.

So the seasons went by with just about every game or fad being played. Funnily enough, each season seemed to take off and end at around the same time every year, like a calendar year.

Knuckle-bone or knuckle-jack time was great. This was

considered a girl's game and boys weren't a threat to us. We played on the school verandahs before school, at playtime and at lunchtime. Whoever went home for lunch made sure they came back early so that they could play a game or two before the bell rang. Little girls learned from the big girls and when they knew how to play properly, the cheeky little things dared to challenge their 'teachers'. 'Huh! Who do you think you are? Get lost, you little bodies,' was a typical reply.

Some girls bought the plastic knuckle-jacks from the shops but the rest of us waited until we had a mutton leg joint for dinner and asked for the bone. All of Broome relied on the cargo ships to bring lamb and mutton from Perth and you had to be pretty quick to buy yours because they'd be gone like greased lightning. Sometimes, a couple of my friends would 'patch up' their knuckles until we had a set of five bones so that we could play a game. We could borrow the bones and we all took turns in minding them overnight, making sure to bring them back the next day. I collected as many bones as I could from my aunties, so that eventually we'd all have a set each. Coloured pencils or crayons were used to paint the bones but with little success, the colour wearing off after a couple of days. Come end of season they'd be chucked in a drawer and forgotten until the following year or our little brothers and sisters would lose them somewhere. It never seemed to bother us when we repeated the whole process of collecting bones in the next year.

I dreaded 'lecky-band' time. Naturally, it was always the boys who started the 'lecky-band' fights. They used the elastic or rubber bands, stretched between the forefinger and thumb to fire the paper pellets to sting us on our arms and legs, sometimes our faces. Boy, it stung. After the boys started the fights, the girls wanted revenge too, for having been stung by them, sometimes for no reason at all. In no time at all, the whole school was involved in the fights. No matter how many times the lecky-bands were banned from school, there was always the sneaky ones who still used them on us, hardly ever being caught.

After the bell sounded each morning the children gathered in front of the big school, as it was called, in readiness for the morning drill.

The school building itself consisted of one very large room with verandahs all around. It was built on concrete stilts about six feet off the ground. The large doors and windows were kept open so that the sea breeze could cool the inside. There were no walls to divide the classes, not even moveable ones. There were only a couple of aisles down the room to separate the lower and upper primary classes. We didn't have one teacher to a class like they do now, for the Sisters took multiple classes under trying conditions. Don't ask me how they managed us all.

We kind of knew what was going on in all the classes. Everyone could hear what was going on from one end of the room to the other. If some kid got into trouble for any little thing, all we had to do was look in the direction of the teacher and we'd know who he or she was and why they got into trouble.

At morning drill we were controlled by Sister Ignatius' silver whistle. We knew all the whistle signals off by heart. We had to stand to attention at arm's length to do the exercises. It was like a regular military drill, with arms and bodies bending this way and that way at the sound of the whistle. Then the marching music would be turned on, this time with legs and bodies right-turning and left-turning, marching us right up on the verandah for routine morning inspection. Every child was made to stand straight and firm, eyes front, chest out, stomachs in, hands to the sides and feet together. Everyone had to be clean and tidy in their clothes and person. It didn't matter if the clothes were old so long as they were clean. Most of us were in bare feet so there was no need for shoes inspection. If anyone wasn't up to scratch the whole school would know. If that child had a tear in her dress and Sister would tell her to have it mended, we'd start giggling and pinching each other, whispering that she had a 'broken' dress. If a boy happened to get into trouble for something or other, he'd be reprimanded and made to feel shame. Everybody laughed out loudly like silly little fools, not knowing any better.

Almost the same routine went on for fingernail inspection. Our arms had to be extended so that Sister could have a good look at our hands and nails. We had to stand in that position until Sister reached us, then we could let them hang by our sides. Relief! The nails had to be clean with no dirt under them. They had to be short and trimmed neatly. One speck of dirt under our nails had us gritting our teeth because we knew that we'd have no time to clean them, no time to look for small straws or splinters on the wooden floors to clean them. In a couple of seconds we'd feel the hard little stick come down on our fingertips ever so swiftly. It would only sting for a little while but that didn't stop us from blowing on our nails and telling everyone it didn't hurt at all, just like a big shot. Sometimes there'd be some snickering down the line with someone saying, 'Good job. Good job.' Somehow it didn't occur to us to complain to our parents. It was punishment for dirty nails and that was that.

The other form of punishment was getting a couple of cuts on our hands or legs and boxed around our ears. As soon as Sister said 'Hands out,' we'd put our hands out but when the rod came down we'd quickly pull our hands back and that would make Sister lose patience. In the end she'd win. Of course there were some kids who did report the punishment to their parents but only a few came to the school to chase it up.

Breathing exercises shortly followed the nail inspection.

'Breathe in deeply through your nose,' Sister said, slowly counting to ten, waving the little hard stick like an orchestral conductor. 'Hold your breath,' she said, holding the stick in mid-air. It seemed like a hundred minutes.

'Breathe out slowly through your mouth and relax,' she finally said. We did that about twenty times, it seemed, before we marched into the classroom.

When Sister Catherine came to teach us in 1952, we found out that one of the things she detested most was chewing gum. It was banned at school. She told us almost every day about her disgust in seeing anyone chewing that rubbish, with their mouths and gums gaping wide open, slapping away, going a mile a minute, like they were having a big race between themselves.

'Good gracious. Look at you. It makes you look like cows and bullocks chewing cud. Jaws, jaws, jaws, mouths are going like bullocks.' That was her catch phrase whenever she caught kids in the playground at recess and made them get rid of it. I was to hear that from Gubinge, Sister's nickname, for the rest of my days at St Mary's.

Sister Catherine was a tough cookie in anybody's books, I'd reckon. She had her rules and, by golly, they were to be obeyed. She was sharp as razors, mouth and mind, hardly missing a trick whenever we got up to mischief or just mucking around. Once, during an afternoon class, Sister happened to look up and caught someone's jaws in action. After months of preaching about the distasteful chewing gum habit, she actually found a defiant young lady in her midst.

'Young lady' she called. 'Come here at once.'

We all looked up from our work as the culprit walked towards her desk. She was a very tall, lean girl who lived at the orphanage and she towered over Sister.

'Yor-yor. She's gonna get it from Gubinge,' someone had whispered quite loudly and we all began to laugh, trying to hide our shaking shoulders from Sister. If she caught us, we'd be next in line at her desk.

'Have you got chewing gum in your mouth, young lady?'

No answer. Tears began welling up in her eyes and the boys in front looked back, giving us the 'she's in trouble' look. We sat up straight in our chairs, sensing that there was more to come.

'I will ask you again. Have you got chewing gum in your mouth, young lady?'

There was still no answer. By this time we began nudging each other right down the line of desks, ready to laugh. We were holding our breaths in anticipation. Answer her, I said in my mind. Answer her.

'I want you to give me the gum. I saw you chewing it.'

Sister must have lost patience with her because the next thing we knew, she went across and made the girl open her mouth and take the chewy out. Sister then stretched the chewy and stuck it on the girl's forehead, turned her around to face us where we, like silly chooks, started laughing.

'This is no laughing matter. This is only an example of you who do not heed rules.' We knew she meant business.

Another time, my cousin Aggie was caught standing on

her seat doing some antics when Sister had her back facing us. Without turning around, she said, 'Hold it right there, Miss Sesar. Stay in that position until I say it's time to sit.'

We were stunned. How could she have seen Aggie? We laughed as usual, seeing Aggie standing there with her arms raised above her head. She stood there for about ten minutes in that position.

When I was in Class 4, learning was getting a little harder, much harder than Class 3. It was good for me because I saw it as a challenge and loved trying to solve the arithmetic problems, getting the hang of the harder English and history lessons.

The day's English lesson was written on the blackboard by Sister Marietta. It was usually written and underlined in this way:- Analyse the following sentences: and they would be numbered in order. Sister would go over one example and then away we'd go. The lessons went on for about a couple of weeks and one afternoon, when doing homework, I asked Mum, who was working away in the kitchen, 'What does analyse mean, Mum?'

'Ask your teacher,' she replied. No more questions. I was happy with the answer.

Next day at school after I read the lessons on the board, I asked Sister Marietta about them and she obliged. This went on for a couple of months and one day she told the class, 'You children should be more like Betty. If you can't understand the lesson, ask as many questions as you like. That way you'll get along with your work.'

She then turned to me asking, 'How come you're the only one asking so many questions, Betty?'

'My mum told me to. She said that analyse was to ask your teacher.' Sister only smiled and went on to finish the lessons.

We had no individual dictionaries and when I finally browsed through an older girl's dictionary out of curiosity and checked the word analyse, I felt so embarrassed about it. I took it for granted and in good faith about Mum's answer. I didn't realise that my poor mum was just telling me to ask Sister what it meant and that she didn't know either. It was a very long time before the penny dropped. Oh dear.

In 1953 there was talk about a camp school being held in the Kimberley, the most likely host town being Broome in 1954, as Port Hedland had already held one for that region. I had been to Port Hedland several times with my Mimi Alice when she visited my other aunties who lived there so I was glad when Broome was chosen. It was an ideal location for camp schools.

It was an exciting time, with the whole town getting involved in some way. Both local schools and the teachers were working together. At meetings, parents and community people were told what was going to happen and so volunteers were allocated jobs such as group leaders right down to the kitchen help and laundry help or whatever came to be.

It was decided that the state school grounds were to be used for the campsite. There was much work to be done like modifying the classrooms into kitchen and dining areas. Being only young people ourselves, we never gave thought to the hard work going on behind the scene. We only looked forward to the fun things we thought were going to happen. Little did we know that it was school as usual, plus whatever else was on the program.

The big day finally arrived and curious kids and grown-ups, on foot and bikes, flocked to the airport to get a good look at the visitors. Several flights arrived from different directions. They were indeed a mixed group of school children, all shapes, sizes and colours. There were only a handful that we recognised; the rest were strangers. That night I could not sleep, thinking about the days ahead.

Each morning the selected camp school kids assembled at St Mary's and marched in single file and in orderly fashion to the state school. All the way to the camp school we were told to march smartly.

'Eyes front! Pull your shoulders back, head straight and no slouching! Don't drag your feet and march in time!' That was our Gubinge, being her usual self. Some of the other kids muttered under their breaths to mimic Sister, just to make the rest of us laugh. We giggled and pinched each other all the way to the camp, making sure that Sister wouldn't catch us in the act.

We had been told to behave, listen to the teachers and be kind to the other children, the visitors and to the state school kids. That part hurt. We couldn't believe that we'd actually be going into enemy territory to see what their school looked like inside. In our minds we thought that because the two schools were rivals (deadly enemies), the teachers would be enemies as well, but not as deadly. What an eye opener the camp school turned out to be! We couldn't believe that a couple of our Sisters and our principal would actually converse with the enemy teachers, nodding and smiling together like one big happy family. Traitors, we grumbled amongst ourselves, to think that they could betray us!

It was not all fun and games like we imagined. It was still work and learning but under a different setting in the open air, under the sprawling poinciana and golden shower trees.

What I liked most was the nature study lessons, learning survival skills and the swimming and diving lessons to gain certificates in the different levels or achievement. Because there were no swimming pools in Broome, we had to rely on the tidal flow for lessons and exams. On one trip to the lighthouse, we were taken to see the dinosaur footprints on the rocks. They could only be seen when it was spring tide and the sea floor was exposed.

After the first day of the camp school, we hung around our new-found friends and relatives to swap stories and jokes. Many of us discovered that we were related to each other just by telling each other about our background. So when we went back home we told our mums and dads about our new relatives. Of course they got very excited too and went back with us to the camp in the evening, trying to find our more about their people in the Halls Creek and Wyndham regions. They were all very surprised and happy to learn that the people in the East Kimberley never forgot those who were taken away. They kept the stories alive so that their descendants knew about the lost ones. Not all were completely lost, thank goodness. Even if our grandparents never caught up with their families who were left behind, at least we'd have made that connection for them through the Kimberley camp school.

One of the biggest events during the camp was the sports day. All the schools had to compete and we had to train hard for the different events. All the other schools wore smart sports uniforms such as shorts and singlets or tops. Being a Catholic school (in those days, especially), we were told from day one that we had to wear our regular school colours of blue and white but instead of the usual blue skirts and white tops, we were to wear white tops and big, blue, elastic-legged Bombay bloomers. No way were we to wear shorts. Talk about uproar! We told the

Sisters that we'd be the only school wearing Bombay bloomers and we'd look stupid. We got no support from the boys, either. It was okay for them; they could wear shorts. Sister Catherine wouldn't budge. We begged the other Sisters to plead on our behalf but they had to follow orders even if they had felt sorry for us. Poor old Holy Rosary students from Derby were in the same boat as us. They had to wear big, green Bombay bloomers. They also begged their Sister but to no avail.

On the day of the sports, all the girls planned to bring blue shorts in case Sister changed her mind (we were still hopeful). Derby and Broome convent schoolgirls still begged until the last minute but Sister still did not relent. The more we pleaded the more she stood by her decision. We turned to Sister Marietta.

'Please Sister. Please Sister. Ask Sister Catherine for us. She'll listen to you,' we begged. When we got no answer, we knew we were defeated and deflated. Our heads hung low on our chests. Somehow, we knew we had no choice but to run in our Bombays, never mind that we were all feeling shame. I think that some of the bigger girls talked us into giving the crowd our best shot and we went on to do just that. Surprisingly, no one laughed at us.

Every year at St Mary's, we held an annual concert, whether it was a Christmas pageant, an adapted play from famous playwrights or musicals.

We thought of how lucky the children were to be chosen for the lead actors and actresses. I had never been chosen to play a lead role, only oneliners that I forgot anyway and was quickly passed over to the next actor's lines. It was over in seconds. No one noticed the blunder, only me, and I kicked myself hard for being so stupid and so miscued. There can be no repeats in live plays as I soon found out.

One year we performed Snow White. Sid Tolentino and Elsa Roe played the leading man and lady, and Gladys Roe played the wicked witch. We rehearsed our parts for weeks and the rumour around the school was that Sid was going to actually kiss Elsa to wake her up. That was the highlight of the year. We never witnessed a kissing scene at school before and we were all excited. Gee, only film stars did that.

Rehearsals came and went but no kissing. How utterly disappointing! The older kids told us that the two would be allowed to kiss on the opening night. Excitement overcame us again. We were on tenterhooks. This time we all crowded around the doors, jammed up like sardines, to wait for the moment. But it never came and we grumbled all the way home. We felt like deflated balloons because we really believed the older kids.

Another year Sister Marietta taught us ballet for a concert that was planned for the end of year. Most little girls dream of being ballerinas and so did we but they were only dreams, besides, who taught ballet for a living in Broome and for what purpose? There were no dance studios in town. We were all excited at the prospect and rushed home with the news and told our mothers that they had to put in the orders for ballet slippers and tap-dancing things. We were going to be ballet dancers, fancy that!

In the meantime, we all rehearsed and practised, boys and girls together until we got it down to a T. Between Sister Marietta, Sister Cecilia and Sister Ignatius we knew that the concert was going to be a huge success, with the dancing, music and gymnastics. The costumes were gorgeous and the older girls danced in the Pink Lady act. Eileen Matsumoto was the Pink Lady and she and the other girls looked stunning in their costumes and points.

The boys looked very handsome and smart in their whites. Sister Ignatius trained them to perfection. We all marvelled at their feats and held our breaths when the smaller boys got on top of the pyramid, hoping nobody would fall and cause the pyramid to collapse.

Sister Marietta also taught the boys and girls tap dancing. I can still hear the tap, tap, tapping of the boys dancing the Sailor's Hornpipe and such. It's such a pity that they did not have video cameras then.

I could run out of pages naming the girls and boys who were students of the three talented nuns and who were also very, very talented. They were solid, those nuns. Teaching us wasn't just a job for them. It was in their hearts and souls, this lifetime dedication to missionary life amongst Aboriginal people.

Thanks to Sister Cecilia, everything went smoothly. Those three nuns made a great team and were a bonus for Aboriginal kids of that era. They made a difference in our lives.

It was around that time when Sister Ignatius took us for choir practice. It was usually Sister Cecilia who did but when she was unavailable Sister Ignatius took over. As usual we were all placed in rows with the little ones in front and bigger ones in the back. I was in the middle row and could see Sister walking back and forth, in time with the music and our eyes following her every movement. She had her hand cupped behind her ear and as we sang she kept walking up and down until we stopped singing.

'There is a man amongst you girls,' she said and we all turned around looking for him. 'There is a deep voice coming from you girls. Now who is it?'

Someone pointed at me and I thought that I was going to cop it, feeling embarrassed about my voice. I was bracing myself for the onslaught. Instead, she said, 'That's all right, Betty. You are an alto contralto in the making.'

What was that? Was that good or bad? I always thought that I had a flat, ugly voice and here was Sister telling me that I had a fine voice for a young girl. She should have said there was a girl with a deep voice amongst us, not giving us a fright about a man. Anyway that alto contralto voice never got me into the charts. I had no ambition to be an opera singer.

We also had very good school picnics organised by the Sisters especially when Sister Ignatius took us into the bush and taught us about nature study and the local environment. This was better than reading about nature in the classroom. We saw live creatures and animals out there. She knew just about every bird call and animal sound of the Australian bush. We had picnics in the bush and seaside alternating every year. They were great times.

Another thing that played a big part in our lives was comic books. Everybody read comics. Sister Catherine told us time and time again that comics weren't proper reading and they would put bad ideas into our heads. We didn't see any evil, only heroes and do-gooders, people who fought crime, people like Dick Tracy, Captain Marvel, Flash Gordon, Superman and the Phantom—the Ghost Who Walks. We were soon to be entering our teens and us girls were forever reading the *Archie* comics and *Photoplay* magazines. None of us could stand Veronica Lodge, the spoilt, little rich girl and just loved it when Betty Cooper had a 'win' over her. As for *Photoplay*, we couldn't wait for it to hit the bookstands.

By this time we were drooling over the new young rising stars such as Tab Hunter, Rock Hudson and Robert Wagner, forgotten were John Wayne, Jeff Chandler, Tony Curtis and Ricardo Montalban. We were famous for matchmaking the young stars and we'd begin pairing off Debbie Reynolds and Tab Hunter, Natalie Wood and Robert Wagner and all those kinds of things. At least Natalie and Robert did marry but we got the shock of all shocks when Debbie Reynolds married Eddie Fisher.

We'd write to their fan clubs in the United States and treasured their pin-up photos on receipt of our fan mail to them. We'd save magazines and newspaper clippings of the stars, keep tabs on the scandalous love affairs of Frank Sinatra and Ava Gardner and their not-so-secret rendezvous around the world, the beautiful, violet-eyed Elizabeth Taylor and her current husband of the time and who would one day take Eddie from Debbie, her supposed best friend. So that was how we spent some of our time, simply reading the comics and film star magazines.

I was mad over comics. Any spare money was spent on them. I would swap them for other comics and save my own favourites to read another day. This comic mania got me into hot water many, many times. Best of all was the fact that my aunties, especially Aunty Peggy, always bought comics and other magazines and handed them over to me when they were finished with them.

When we were in Class 6, a few of the 'outside kids' started skipping Friday afternoon classes so that we could read all our favourite comics at a friend's house, Sally's and Pearly's house, to be exact. This went on for a few weeks, until Sister caught on to us. The same girls were disappearing from classes every Friday afternoon. She put two and two together and it sure didn't come up fives. When confronted about this, we couldn't deny it because nobody but nobody ever lied or attempted to lie to any of the Sisters, especially Sister Catherine. She didn't punish us in the usual way on this occasion but left it to our parents to sort it out. With Sister, it would have only been a couple of cuts across our thumbs, open palmed, or on the backs of our legs. It would have been over in a couple of minutes. With my Mum, it was being being constantly ear-bashed about my naughtiness and the shame I brought to her, day in and day out, for the next couple of months or so. I sure missed going to the pictures and beaches. Never again did I miss Friday afternoon classes nor did any of the others. We were on our honour not to do this again.

Through reading comics and the newspapers, I developed an appetite for reading sensible books, from short stories to novels and historical literature. I loved reading and would read just about anything placed in front of me. When there wasn't any reading material around I would line up the kitchen table with the large Sunshine milk tin, jam jar, the different packages of dry goods and read their labels until I knew them off by heart. My mum thought that I was quite mad, just staring at the tins and jars. We weren't allowed to read at the table during meals and she soon removed all the tins and jars from the table, when she finally woke up to what I was doing. I would even read the mail-order catalogues and knew every shoe style, dress style and colours of the season.

I still read the occasional comics that I find in my children's rooms. Whenever I do read the comics, I stop a while and think about my own time as a comic-mad kid and my eyes begin to water. I am still a movie fanatic and whenever I go into the city, I spend my leisure time haunting the cinemas that are a far cry from the open air theatre of my childhood era: the Sun Picture theatre.

Another thing that I must mention is that I read a lot of English storybooks such as the *Famous Five* and *Secret Seven* series. I was a bit envious of the fun those kids had, even though they were only stories. When I look back, we had a lot of fun and adventure, too, as kids.

Despite my antics at school, Sister Catherine gave an excellent school report about me to the Bishop and I was requested to have an audience with him at Beagle Bay in December of 1956.

FATHER
BISHOP

ONE DAY, BEFORE THE CHRISTMAS SCHOOL BREAK in December of 1956, Mum told me that the Most Reverend Bishop Otto Raible wanted to see me in Beagle Bay and Father Kevin McKelson would arrange for me to go there with Brother William on the mission truck. Mum didn't know much about the details involving the audience but she did mention that the Bishop was thinking about sending someone to Perth to a boarding school.

Everyone stood to attention when the Bishop's name was mentioned. I was always in awe of this grand old gentleman Bishop. I remembered him well, mostly as a child living in Beagle Bay and whenever he had to come to Broome on official visits. Even though Broome was his official residence, he preferred to live in Beagle Bay with his people.

On the day I arrived, I was told by Sister Therese to go and see the Bishop in his little office at the back of the church. I was weak in the knees and felt a bit squirmy in the tummy. I'd never had an audience with the Bishop or any Bishop for that matter. As children we gathered around him in groups to ask for his blessing and to kiss the ring. He was very friendly and always had time to talk to us even though we couldn't understand him too well with his German accent. Smaller kids tried to reach up and touch his great big beard, while the bigger ones followed him, taking out their rosary beads, small statues and holy pictures for him to bless. Talking to him on my own was a different story though but after a while I felt at ease. I felt so small sitting in the large padded chair, facing him and looking at his long flowing beard. I couldn't look at him directly so I just focused on his beard.

He asked me all the normal questions such as: Did I like school, did I enjoy the lessons and what did I think about higher education?

'I have heard that you are quite bright at school but then I have always known that my native people have brains like everyone else, in size, weight and colour. They can be educated like the white people if given a chance. The Native Affairs people know about you too because they keep in contact with the schools. I have asked you to come to talk with me about such matters.'

Being older seemed to make me understand his English a little better than before and I suppose it was because I was so anxious to find out the complete details of his proposal that I may have wanted to make myself understand him.

Did I want to go? Did I know what it was all about? Did I know that I wouldn't see my family during the year and would be away for almost a year? He seemed to know a lot about the homesickness whole families suffered whenever anyone had to go away. Did I have any idea what living in a boarding school was like? Would I be able to cope with the conditions and the studies? No, I didn't know what it was all about but I would try it because it was something I always dreamed about, always knowing it was out of reach for native people. Opportunity only knocks once, in my books, anyway.

I told him that I would like to go but where was the money coming from? My family didn't have any and there were no scholarships unless you went to a state school, so we were told.

'Do not worry about that, child. Go home and talk it over with all your mothers. Let me know through Father McKelson but don't leave it too late because you will have to leave in late January or early February. The good Sisters have contacted the Dominican Ladies College in Dongara, St Gertrude's in New Norcia, St Brigid's College in Lesmurdie and Iona Presentation College in Mosman Park. Sister Catherine will have all the brochures for you to look at.'

We chatted for about an hour and then I left. His parting words stayed with me forever and were words to this effect.

'I have a great vision for our people. I can see them getting a good education and holding good jobs and becoming doctors and lawyers. You are seen as a race of people having no brains and can't do anything for yourselves, in the white man's eyes. I know differently because I have been here with your people, who are also my people, for many, many years and know them as very clever people. I would like to establish a centre to educate our Aboriginal children in higher education and training but we can only start in small numbers. I am pleased that you will give it a try. If all goes well, I hope to send more children down to Perth.'

Over the years, I often thought about what he was telling me. I understood him, but I have learned a lot more since about the perceived differences between intellectual races and who were supposedly superior.

Many white people believed that Aboriginals were an inferior race and on an intellectual scale were on the lowest rung.. This belief was supported by scientists in the earlier times who thought that each race was at a different level. They believed that Europeans (white blood) were the most highly evolved, then followed by the Asian races and so forth, leaving the Australian Aboriginal the last.

It came to this: that white blood was more superior, black blood was inferior. Some authoritative people believed that because the half-caste or quarter-caste children had white blood these children could be educated like the white people and have a fair chance in life, as far as education and employment go.

I had heard some nuns and other white people say almost the same thing. In school there were comments like: 'Of course the coloured children do better at school because they have mixed blood in them' and 'Most of them seem to grasp maths problems easier than the rest.' We were led to believe that, until we knew better: we were not dumb.

The white race in dealing with the dark race seems always to think of Aboriginal people as subhuman or outcasts of society. Someone mentioned to me once, that it stands to reason that white blood is considered stronger because children from black and white parents are born fair and keep getting fairer as they integrate with whites. They don't throw back. So they must use the same reasoning for our intelligence levels.

I didn't think of myself as a guinea pig being tested for the educational intelligence level of native people. I knew that I could do it and saw it as an opening round victory for us, so that other children could have the opportunity to be educated at a higher level, not finishing school in Class 5 or 6. I was not pressured into going away for schooling. I wanted to go.

I thought that if I survived almost three years in an orphanage without my mum and dad, surely I could survive for a few years longer in another environment. I was older now.

Outside the church, I threw my arms and hands in the air and danced around the place. I was so excited that I wanted to let Mum know right then but it wasn't possible as we had no phone at home or here on the mission. I couldn't wait to get back to Broome to tell them all. On the other hand I wanted to stay for another week with my mission mob. So I stayed and went back to Broome just before Christmas.

I had to sleep in the girls' dorm for the duration of my stay but was free to visit the colony to see my relations during the day. Sometimes I took afternoon rest with the other girls in the dorm and enjoyed it immensely, the girl talk and those kinds of things.

One day after the midday meal in the dining hall, we went

back to the dorm to rest up. My little cousin, Patricia Paddy, who was called Budja, came to sit on my bed and we started telling stories but quietly. Several other girls were sitting on my bed as well as sitting on the floor. While I was having my hair brushed, Budja wormed her way to sit near me and showed me her closed fist. She was only about nine and I was her big sister at fourteen.

'Jidja Betty, look what I got. My mummy gave me some chicken and look what I found. I saved it to show you,' said Budja.

'Well, show me then. What have you got there?'

She opened her small palm and nestled in it was a chicken's heart.

'You see that little heart? It came from the chooky fowl and you see all the little black spots on it? Well, that's the chooky fowl's sins. It must've been a really naughty chooky fowl.'

She said it so sweetly and so seriously that I couldn't tell her that animals don't have souls. The other girls just rolled over and laughed and laughed, going into a fit frenzy. In the end, Budja and I joined in the laughing because it became too contagious to ignore. She didn't know what was going on. After about ten minutes of tummy cramps, someone did manage to tell Budja about the chooky fowl's heart and that they don't have souls. She took it okay. I was only glad it wasn't me who told her.

'Thank goodness I didn't show it to Sister. I'd feel shame telling her about it.'

During my stay there, my Aunty Lydia and Uncle Billy Lawford took me fishing and hunting. They had their own little ones and we all walked to the fishing spots or the bigger boys gave us a ride

DONKEYS AT BEAGLE BAY, 1958

on their bikes, dropping us there and riding back to pick up the other kids.

Along the way we stopped for water at one of the water springs and had a good drink to refresh ourselves. I remembered the springs from when I was much smaller and they hadn't changed much. Even now I can smell the ti-trees and marsh in my mind.

On one mixed outing with the dormitory kids, we spotted some donkeys and the boys caught them so that we could have rides in turns. There were two or three girls astride on each donkey but the animals didn't seem to mind. It was a real fun day for me and for the others, I suppose, because it wasn't too often that there were mixed outings. Sometimes the donkeys ran for a good distance and other times they just stood there and wouldn't move an inch, not even when prodded. At one stage I jumped off and walked away with the other girls.

There were wild fruit and nuts around and we picked some to eat. Nearby, we saw some cattle milling around the shady trees and some were lying around with their calves. After about twenty minutes, someone was yelling at us to get moving because the cattle were going to stampede. I don't know whether we frightened them or not but we didn't wait to find out. Aunty Chrissy Kelly and Aunty Margaret Yumbi grabbed one hand each and pulled me away with them, at the same time getting whipped in our faces by the twiggy branches and scratched by the underbrush. The cattle were pounding towards us and the only thing we could do was to climb up a skinny young tree that only had about five or six strong branches.

Aunty Chrissy pushed me onto the higher branch while she stood on the lower one, clinging to dear hope. Goodness knows how Aunty Madeline got up as there were four other girls hanging on. I don't know how that tree held all of us but it did. When the stampede was over we just sat in the dust and laughed our silly heads off.

I had to go back home within the next few days and it was sad to leave because I knew that I'd be gone for a year and probably wouldn't see the mission people again for another couple of years. There were quite a few tears when Brother William pulled away from the mission. Goodbye, my mission family, I thought, all the way to Broome.

When I got home, I told Mum what the audience with Father Bishop was all about. I said that I wanted to go away and sit for the Junior Certificate and if possible, the Leaving Certificate. I wanted to become a teacher and come back to Broome to teach. I knew that it was going to be hard slogging for I only did the first year of secondary school by correspondence and was helped by Sister Catherine. It wasn't the same as being in a classroom with a teacher right in front of you, every day. I had to wait for about three to four weeks for my work to be marked and mailed back.

Thank goodness for Sister Catherine. She was all brains and I could not have done it without her. She was one of those Sisters who firmly believed in Aboriginal children being just as brainy as anyone else.

READY FOR PERTH

I THINK EVERYONE KNEW that I'd be going away for schooling the following year. Mum bought me a huge suitcase for all the things I had to take with me, even my own linen and blankets. I set about getting all my clothes marked right down to my socks and jowidge.

My Aunty Peggy bought me my first camera, a Brownie box camera. I never owned a camera before, only used my friends' cameras to take pictures. I was so thrilled. Aunty Peggy had a string of kids and she was good fun. She was the only aunty who could drive a car and boy, did we go everywhere in it. The kids packed into it like sardines, heads sticking out but we didn't give a hoot. Just about every day one could see her with Tracey Cox and my very good friend Olive Gurry at Aunty Mary's and Uncle Phillip Cox's place, just down the road from us. Their place was like a second home to me. Tracey, Olive and I were always surrounded by our brothers and sisters, minding them and playing with them in that big yard of theirs. Years later that big yard of theirs was packed with huge, shady mango trees and everyone knew it as Mango Tree and gathered there whenever and anytime.

Of course, I made time to spend with my other friends at their homes or down the front beach, swimming until we were burnt blacker than our own skins from the hot sun and salty sea. The usual skylarking and *goolmudjing* went on too, for weren't we all teenagers? There were wolf whistles galore at the beach for us teenagers or even when walking down the streets around town. It was good fun when we were in a group for we teased ourselves by nudging each other and saying, 'That was for you, jidja. You must have IT.' Talk about skiting!

Anyway, it was sad in a way to leave my family and friends. They all knew that I wouldn't be back for May and August holidays and they all promised to write to me to ease the loneliness ahead.

I knew by then that two schools had accepted me but I chose St Brigid's in Lesmurdie. I would be outfitted with the uniforms when I arrived there, I was told.

The big day arrived and the small airport was packed with parents, friends and other children going away to boarding schools or going back home to Perth or going to the school camp at Point Peron. It was a direct flight to Perth, no stopovers. On the silver DC3 it would take ages to get there but still a shorter time than by stopping at every airport down the coastline. Seeing my family and friends together all at the same time, I got emotional and very weepy even though I was both happy and sad. It suddenly hit me that I wouldn't be seeing them again for a very long time.

Previously, I had been chosen to go to the camp school first and then St Brigid's but was told by Sister Catherine that it was out of the question. School came first. Two nuns would wait for my arrival, one of them being Sister Raymond whom I knew.

There was a bit of confusion at Guildford Airport when we disembarked and collected our baggage. The camp school officials were there to greet us and as they were checking the list, my name was called out. I thought that Sister may have changed her mind and allowed me to go to the camp. I could see no sign of Sister Raymond or her companions and that sent my hopes up higher. So after waiting for about ten minutes more to give the Sisters a little time to get there, the officials decided that they would take me with them into the city to meet the Daily News press, and a message was left at the counter for the nuns, just in case they came looking for me. No way was I going to wait at the airport by myself.

In the city the *Daily News* newspaper was waiting for us. I suppose it was a good storyline, children from remote areas coming to the 'big smoke' for the first time, getting the chance of a lifetime to go to a summer camp for nearly two weeks. We talked to them and they took some photos of us looking up to the tall buildings that weren't really tall. Anyway, we thought it was great being photographed.

Just as we were about to hop onto the bus, the two nuns arrived and after speaking to the camp officials, they promptly whisked me away in their car to go to the Pallottine Centre in Riverton to see Father John Lumen.

'I'm afraid you won't be going to the camp school, my dear. You've come here to learn and learn you will. It won't be too bad up there. You'll meet other young girls and make friends and you'll be able to see the city from your window,' said Sister Raymond who was also one of my former teachers in little school.

I was to stay at the Pallottine Centre for a couple of days until school opened and Father was to take me up to St Brigid's in the hills to meet the Reverend Mother Celestine and the Sisters of Mercy staff. It must have taken us about two hours to find the Pallottine Centre because it was one of the newer suburbs and it looked as if the two old girls hadn't brought a map. Finally, after asking for directions, we pulled up at the Pallottine Centre where we met Father Lumen and Miss Edith Little.

There were some other kids there who were also waiting for school to open. They were from down south. We were the first lot of kids to be brought to the city schools to receive secondary education. The Bishop's great plan was slowly getting under way, with a handful of kids coming from the missions and schools run by the Pallottine Society.

It was a fairly good weekend for me at 'Pallo', which was going to be called just that by all of us. Edie kept me occupied with things to do until they took me up to the hills. The few boys who were there were day scholars and boarded in the limited rooms available. Many years down the track, the student residential buildings were erected for the boys and girls who came from all over the state. A small playing field separated the boy's dorm from the girl's dorm.

It was a very pleasant drive to St Brigid's. The gradual incline to the hilly country was a treat for me because I had never been on mountain ranges, ever. The whole countryside was different, a softer looking environment with strange green trees and rocky slopes. The scrubby density of bush land up north was indeed so very different to the huge trees and ground growth of the hills. I could only drink in the scenery with my eyes and savour the fresh mountain air with my nose.

The front driveway of St Brigid's was finally in sight and

ST BRIGID'S COLLEGE, 1950s

looked a bit grand to me. It was semi-circled with an entrance at both ends and a spectacular show of roses galore adorning the frontage. Roses were my favourite flowers even though I had only seen them in magazines and movies. I was aching to touch their velvety petals and promised myself I'd do that whenever I had the chance.

We were shown into the waiting room and waited for Mother Celestine to come and meet with us. I didn't know what to expect when Mother walked in. I got a surprise when this tiny woman in black robes and veil entered the room. She couldn't have been bigger than me and looked smaller again when she stood beside Father Lumen. I just sat back and looked on when she and Father began talking. I was then taken to the Sub-Juniors dorm where I was to live for the rest of the year and then Father and I went on a guided tour of the place. Soon it was dinner time and Father had to take his leave, promising that he'd pick me up for the Easter break so that I could spend it with the other kids there.

That night in the Sub-Juniors dorm, the girls gave me the run-down of the house rules, what to do and what not to do. I tried to remember as much as I could because the rules were too many to take in for one night.

The Sub-Juniors dorm was shared with some of the Class 7 boarders because there were only a handful of Sub-Juniors (Class 8) boarders. They were Myra Swan, Anne Rijavec, Eva Pinchin, Teresa Vavra, Pauline Keating (whose brother Michael was studying to be a priest), Mary Coffey and Andrea Soord who hadn't arrived from Sarawak as yet. Amongst the Class 7 boarders was Colleen Hickey whose brother Barry was also studying to be a priest. The two brothers went on to become Bishop Keating and Archbishop Hickey.

The first day at school was a shock to me. I hadn't expected to see so many girls attending as day scholars and a number of mixed students in the primary school. I think the boys went there until Class 3 then had to go to either Mary's Mount in Kalamunda or to other primary schools in the city. Busloads of students pulled up at the front and made a beeline to their classrooms to await the bell call.

At assembly, all I could see was a sea of white faces sprinkled with a few brown faces in between. They were the few overseas Asian boarders and I believe that I was the only Aboriginal student who had ever attended the school. Everybody could see that I was neither white nor Asian, from the looks I received in that first week. Even the nuns asked if goats and cattle still ran down the streets and whether the people still rode in donkey drays. I just told myself that I only came to Perth this one time but it was obvious that they (the nuns) had never been up north or heard about our lifestyle. I kind of forgave them for their embarrassing questions and ignorance of our Kimberley country.

In class I was introduced to the day scholars and soon settled down to the class routine. I didn't know what to expect. The class numbers were quite large and we were all in uniforms, black skirts, black stockings and white shirts with the school tie. We all looked quite smart in uniform, I may add. I liked the fact that different teachers came to us for each subject period, instead of having the one teacher who taught all our subjects.

We all made friends very quickly and the day scholars wanted to take me to their homes for weekends but I was a little reluctant to go, being shy with strangers and having never really been to white families' homes before. At first I thought that I may have been a novelty, but later on I found out that they had genuine intentions and wanted to share their homes with me.

Everything looked good on the surface but it was the nights

that were the loneliest. During the first days there I was occupied with school routine, our recreational time after school, the evening rosary, dinner and homework. After that we had to go to the basement to have our baths or showers, polish our shoes for the next day then go to bed. That basement was sure spooky!

It was the hour before sleep would creep into my eyes that was awful for me. After saying our night prayers I just hopped into bed and cried silently every night for almost two months. I dared not cry out loudly because the other girls might think that I was a real sooky baby or that I might start up the other new boarders crying and we'd all get into trouble. So I silently wept for the loss of my family and friends in Broome and Beagle Bay. Big Shot Hero! I called myself that name just about every night.

Of course time does ease the pain and things got a little better. I managed to go into the city a few times and eventually got talked into staying with school friends on some long weekends. I even stopped crying completely before the end of term.

What I found most difficult was to manage time. I just could not manage it. I knew that there was a timetable for the boarders and a timetable for the school lessons and activities. The school timetable was okay because there was only the one classroom for us and for recess and lunch all I had to do was follow the others. I mentioned in the beginning of my story about my always being the last to go to Mass, pulling on my stockings and shoes on the run and being the last one for meals. Well, that was all true but eventually I managed to train or condition myself to be better as the years went by. It was hard but I got by.

The bell woke us up at 5am every morning except when we were privileged with sleep-ins. Sister started clanging the bell and walked up and down the stairs and in front of all the dorms. I didn't know what was happening, watching the girls jump out of bed and getting ready for morning prayers. I dreaded the sound of that bell especially in the winter months, when it was so cold that I didn't want to get out of bed. I felt so sorry for the littlies tucked in their warm beds, only to be woken up in the cold.

In those days there were boarders from Class 1 to Leaving standard. I couldn't get over the fact that parents could put their little ones, from the tender age of six, into such lonely places: most of the littlies lived in the metropolitan areas. The separation of us from our parents on the mission to the dorms was not a choice. How privileged the white parents were to have a choice in sending their children away. They must have had lots of money to keep their children there. I may have been crying for home at age fourteen but can you imagine the crying of those lonely little white babies. I can because I saw them.

I made quite a few friends in our class, boarders and day scholars but it was with the boarders that I felt closest to because we all lived with each other every day, going to Mass in the chapel, sharing our meals and homework and just about every other thing that we did on campus, hiding away in the library and reading volumes and volumes of appropriate reading materials, hanging around the playing field, playing sport or taking off to the corner shop across the road. We weren't allowed to go there without permission but some of us did sneak through the fence, just to get lollies and cool drinks. We could go over there on Saturday afternoons after getting our pocket money from Sister Rose. Whatever money we received from home had to be handed over to the bursar for safety reasons.

All the boarders had their chores whether it was polishing the floorboards or working in the dining room. No slacking off. My chore was the sports change room in the first year and polishing verandahs in the next. Sometimes we swapped with each other.

The first time Mum wired money to Kalamunda Post Office was a day to remember. After getting permission to go with Margaret Anderson, a day scholar and one of my best friends, we made plans on how to get there. The bus timetable didn't work out to our advantage so Margaret said that we could walk. Because I was broke and couldn't wait for the following week, I agreed to go walking into Kalamunda. Margaret knew her way around the traps all right because soon I found my way into the back roads of the hill country. That girl took me up and down the bush tracks and trails, into the small streams, bogging in mud up to our stockinged mid-calves, cutting across people's backyards and finally into the town centre. I told her that if that was the way back, I'd take my chances on the main road but that wasn't necessary for we caught the bus. I had taken off my stockings and wrapped them in a paper bag and had a hard time scraping the mud off my shoes. I made it back in time for dinner but I had to clean up properly and change into a fresh uniform.

The boarders started talking about a retreat that was held every year and it got me interested. I only thought that nuns and priests had retreats, not school kids or ordinary people. Anyway we were told about it by Mother Celestine and had a brief information session on it. Under no circumstances were we to talk to anyone. It was to be a time spent in prayer and meditation, a spiritual time for cleansing of the mind, body and soul.

It started on the Friday after Mass in the chapel and took off with a great start. Before it began we told each other that they weren't to tempt us into talking or even look in each other's direction. We all agreed. My weekend was spent in the library browsing through books or curling up under a shady tree reading them or going to the chapel to pray. Sometimes in passing my friends, I lowered my eyes and kept going. Sometimes I did pair off with a friend just to read or swap a book but we never spoke. There was silence all around the place, even on the playground.

By the end of the weekend it became sheer torture for us to even look at each other. The girls began to write notes, asking how we were coping and writing silly ditties. I tried hand signs and gestures but the others didn't have a clue what I was trying to say. We ended up doubling over and running away from each other to have silent 'laughs' alone. I wasn't cut out for long silences it seemed. All in all it was a very good experience for me and every now and again, at home with my kids, I threaten to go into retreat somewhere out bush because I had experienced the spiritual cleansing of mind, body and soul and the solitude and silence of a retreat. If ever I become a victim of society-related stress, retreat would be the way to go for me for the healing process: no pill popping, medication or electric shock treatment.

There were house rules already in place from years and years ago and they had never been abolished. I agreed with some of them but some were utterly ridiculous. One was that shorts, slacks or jeans were not allowed to be worn because trousers were men's clothing and young ladies should not be seen wearing such clothing items, especially at St Brigid's. Even when we had our annual concerts and when acting in a male's role, no one was allowed to wear costume trousers to act the part. They had to wear their dresses. How utterly ridiculous! It was only a play. How things have changed there now. The boarders can wear just about anything they choose now. How lucky for them.

The other rule was whistling. Catholic ladies never whistle, it is so unbecoming of them. Some of us couldn't even sing in tune or play a musical instrument so we whistled in tune because it was the only way we could express our musical taste. Just like tapping our feet to the rhythm of music because we couldn't dance properly. One day when I was caught whistling a hit tune, I heard loud clapping of hands and looked up to see Sister Evangelus beckoning me. I went to see what she wanted and boy, did I cop a dressing. By the time she finished, I was full bottle on the do's and don'ts of Catholic ladies behaviour in public.

We also had to sit properly with our backs and shoulders straight, hands folded on our laps and legs crossed at the ankles. No sitting with our legs stretched out like cowboys sitting on a fence. There were other silly rules (to us) but we had to abide by them. In those days of the 1950s we did think that some of them were too harsh and we complained (amongst ourselves, of course) that it was worse than a concentration camp.

It was a kind of joke amongst us, calling ourselves prisoners but we weren't. It was just school kid's talk. In reality, the Sisters had a huge responsibility and for all of us and it was their duty of care.

At catechism classes it was drilled into us about the sins of the flesh: adultery, one man–one woman marriage forever. We all learned about the do's and don'ts but when it came to sex education in the fifties it was a total no show. No one spoke about it or even slyly whispered about it amongst the seniors as far as we knew. Even if they thought about it or knew a little bit more than we did, they did not share their knowledge with us in case someone pimped on them. If anyone even attempted to test us on our knowledge, they were threatened that Sister would be told about it. The older girls told us that in time we'd know, that our mothers would tell us, but our mothers never did.

We knew the Ten Commandments, the Seven Cardinal Sins and the Seven Sacraments off by heart, back to front and from start to finish when we were younger, but to discuss openly anything relating to sex was simply not on.

One day, to our surprise, we heard from the older girls that a sex education class was going to be introduced as a trial. We didn't know how it was to be delivered and we were sure curious.

Our class numbered about twenty girls. We didn't know that on this particular day we'd be introduced to our first sex education class. There was no prior warning. Sister came in at the usual time in the morning but we sensed there was something about to happen. She was between sixty and sixty-five years of age, I'd say, probably straight from home, into the convent forever and eventually, out of Ireland, from her very early teens.

Like I said, there was no warning or introduction about this session. Sister just paced up and down the room in front of us, pointing her finger at us as she glided slowly across the room in her long black robes and veil. Later on, after class, we all agreed that she made us shake that morning from head to foot.

'You girls will be aware that your bodies are undergoing a change, physically and that God made man and woman physically different. Others may not be as developed as some of you but will change never the less. So beware!'

We knew about boys being different to girls as most of us had to change nappies and bath our siblings to help out at home but we didn't know that much.

Sure, we did notice that our bodies were slowly changing physically. We were noticing boys as well and that one day we'd probably start dating when we were old enough. Some of the ethnic girls were betrothed and already knew who their future husbands were to be, even though some had not even set eyes on them as yet, not even photographs. We were like stupid gawks when we saw a few boys lining up for Mass or Benediction. Yes, we were developing waistlines and bustlines too as well as other girl things. I for one didn't know that pain was associated with my growing breasts. It sure was annoying, that stretching of skin and bursts of pain in the centre peaks. Maybe that's where the term 'growing pains' came to be.

'Beware!' she repeated, her finger pointing at each one of us as she kept gliding up and down the room. At each turn she spun around and called out, 'Beware!' in a strong, quaky voice.

We really got frightened now and when Sister wasn't looking at us, we looked at one another and either shrugged or whispered, 'Beware of what?'

Suddenly, Sister had spun around and glared at one little slightly overweight girl. Before we knew it she had snapped the 'B' word at her.

'What do we have to beware of, Sister?' she asked and we could see tears forming in her eyes.

'Beware! Beware of the boneless finger, I say! It could get you into a lot of strife when you least expect it,' she shouted and we all screamed.

'Now open up page twenty,' she said and we all screamed again when we saw what was staring back at us.

'I'll tell my mummy on her,' promised the little plump girl when we got out of class but she never did tell. Sister's words were still ringing in our ears for days to come.

There was another time when the same Sister told us about having a shower.

'Bodies are to be washed or showered every day as you know.

They are temples of your souls and must be treated with respect. So when you wash your bodies with the cake of soap, do not let your hands linger too long on your breasts or especially further down with the soap. It will put evil thoughts, words and actions into your heads,' she said. We were shocked and shaking again.

That next long weekend most of the girls brought back liquid soap, or used their shampoo for soap. Those were only some of the sexual awareness talks we had experienced in class and did we really learn anything from those kinds of lessons? I think not.

Sex education and sexual awareness programs sure weren't delivered as they are now, I'm certain of it. Even though it was modern times then, the 1950s, it was still like the dark ages, when I ponder on such happenings.

Until I was about seventeen, I had never heard about lesbians and homosexuals either. My future husband, John Lockyer, had made a remark to me about my cousin Robin Clarke and my holding hands together as we walked along beside him. His words bothered me for a few days and I kept asking myself what was wrong with him. She was his cousin too, on his mother's side so why was he getting annoyed? All my girl cousins and girl friends held hands whenever we walked together, even three or four of us in a line. We'd been doing that since we were in kindy and big school. It was a girl thing and friendship thing.

It was not until I read a book that the penny dropped. I was shocked and couldn't believe that same sex relationships existed, and it took me a long time to accept. These days even seven-year-olds know more about it than I did. I must have been yarm, all right.

One might even question my being naïve and ignorant of this fact and of my knowledge of the bible history. Yes, we did know about the story of Sodom and Gomorrah but it was never told to us explicitly. I only knew that really bad people, evil to the core, lived against the teachings of God and that angered Him so the two cities were destroyed.

For school holidays and long weekends the college was closed and we had to make arrangements to go home or stay with friends. If I didn't go with friends, Father Lumen picked me up to stay with Edie and the other kids at Pallo. Edie took me to the Coolbara League to dances a couple of times and it was great. She did a few things like that for us kids. It was so tragic when she died at a young age some years later.

In my first year there I stayed with the Luz family in Kojonup whose twin daughters, Marie and Daphne, boarded as well, the Rijavec family from Manjimup whose daughter Anne was in my class and a good friend, and the Heppekausen family from Queen's Park whose daughter Henrieka was also a very good friend of mine, even though she was a year below me and a day scholar. I had many good friends at school and there were a few who were truly close and genuine, and not because I was a native novelty but as a person in my own right. One such person was Mary Coffey. She only boarded for the first term but we became firm friends in that short time even though she was a white girl. Perhaps it was because we both came from the Kimberley; she from Wyndham and I from Broome.

At the Perth Royal Show later in the year, someone grabbed me around the waist then covered my eyes with hands. I thought I was being mugged and screamed out loudly, like a fool. When I was released and spun around to face the person, I saw it was Mary. She had spotted me in the crowd and was so excited to see me that she could only act on impulse. We laughed and cried for a few minutes then walked around talking for a while, catching up on news. Soon it was time to go back with Edie and the others so Mary and I parted once again and shed a few tears. I didn't see her again until we met at a Catholic girls' interschool basketball competition the following year. There was the same reaction as at the Royal Show and it was sad again when we said our farewell. I never saw my friend again in all those years but I often think about her and all those other friends, from time to time.

Staying with the Luz family on their farm was really great. It was a 'first' for me. I had never been on a dairy farm before and I had a strange feeling being there. Maybe it was the different environment, the greenness of the farming country and the farm animals. It was a novelty seeing the dairy cows getting milked and watching Mr Luz calling out to the herd in the evening. They came from all directions of the property at his calling and their bellowing back at him. I was fascinated at the kind of rapport they had between them.

Perhaps that strange feeling was because I was an Aboriginal person from a different 'country' and didn't greet the spirits properly in the traditional way. I didn't know that until I went back home and told Mimi.

They were a good and kind host family for the two weeks that I spent there. The whole family was great, from the two older sons to the younger children. I watched them make their own butter and buttermilk, we had fresh milk every day and everything possible was home made or home grown. I was taken just about everywhere and felt quite at home with them. Mr Luz was quite old but he was fit for his age, doing his share of the farm with Bill and Ray, their sons.

It was very, very cold for me down south with the constant

drizzle, blueless skies and the chills that went right through my body and bones. No matter how many blankets I used, I could never feel warm enough. I couldn't believe it could get so cold. While I wore two jumpers, one short-sleeved one and the regular school jumper over it, other girls just wore the regular jumpers and laughed at me when they saw me shivering. I had chilblains on all of my toes and they itched like blazes. It was sheer agony when wearing regular lace-ups and I couldn't resist taking them off in class, where Sister couldn't see my feet. When the girls told me that the really hot weather would arrive about October or November, I felt so sick at the thought of waiting all those months. There were no heaters in the dorms or classrooms and I just loved it when I went away to friends for holidays because they'd have open fireplaces and warm rooms.

The August holidays found me spending them at Wandering Mission, which was also run by the Pallottines and a German order of nuns. I stayed at the convent with the Sisters but spent the days with the mission kids. It was the coldest place in the country by my standards and if I hadn't walked around the place I'm sure that I would have turned into a human icicle, frozen in the middle of the paddock. There were large open fires lit outside in the evenings and all the kids gathered around, warming their hands and bodies in the heat, until it was bed time. Some of the little girls walked me all the way back to the convent, which was a fair distance away and scary in the dark.

One of the younger girls who followed me around the place in my first few days at Wandering and who became my closest mate there was Marjorie Winmar. I followed her as well because I didn't know anyone else there. She was one of those friendly kids who was constantly smiling and funning about and who would do just about anything for you, within reason, of course.

Anyway, one of the things they did on the mission was to go on walks for miles and miles and look for mushrooms in the fields. It sure was beautiful country around there, pretty cold and wet at that time of the year but it was a strange, exhilarating experience walking in the coldest of temperatures, getting my face frozen and then unfrozen when I eventually got back to the roaring fires of the mission. I didn't know anything about real mushrooms and it was a good learning place for me because I hadn't ever considered eating them at all. I only saw the tinned mushrooms on the shop shelves and they didn't look appealing enough for me to even try them. Thanks to those girls, I had acquired a taste for them but after all that mushroom hunting, I still wouldn't be able to distinguish the edible ones from the non-edibles so I just stick to the fresh one in the supermarkets.

I had a few things going for me in that first year such as basketball competition and hard slogging at school in all my subjects. The boarders went on bushwalks in the hills, day trips to Mundaring Weir, picnics at Lesmurdie Falls and doing our own thing, within reason, in our leisure time. We were taught ballroom dancing which was great and we taught ourselves to rock'n'roll and jive, undercover of course. Some girls had little transistors and we'd listen to the hits and start jiving, always looking out in case any of the Sisters came along because we were not allowed to do any un-ladylike things like rock'n'roll dancing. Sometimes our class did the un-ladylike thing like dancing down in the darkness of the basement area, which was spooky enough during the day, let alone at night.

There were a few loquat trees growing across the road from

us but it was still part of the ground of St Brigid's, only fenced off from the main buildings. As the fruit on them was getting riper, the strong smells were very tempting to us. Every day, the fruit looked bigger and juicier and every day there were dozens of fruit falling and rotting on the ground. I couldn't understand why the Sisters just couldn't give them to us to eat instead of letting them rot away. The fruit were just going to waste.

One night a few of us climbed through a window on the bottom floor and went across the road just to taste the loquats. I climbed the lower branches and reached to pluck the fruit and couldn't wait to taste them. They sure were juicy. Some other girls climbed up the other trees and filled a couple of bags to bring back to the dorm. As we jumped down from the trees a few of us landed on cow's muck and screamed out loudly in disgust. Luckily we had on our sandshoes on because the gravel ground was hard and cold and we had opted to wear them instead of our slippers. We limped back into the grounds looking for a hose to wash our feet and shoes. Goodness, it sure was cold but we stayed until the smell was gone from the shoes. On top of that someone had bolted the windows shut and we had to walk around to the dorm and throw pebbles on the window-pane to get someone to open the downstairs window. Thank goodness no one thought we were blokes trying to break in, otherwise we'd have been rounded up by the police. We went down to the basement, making as little noise so we could scrub our feet and sandshoes with nice smelling soap. I suppose we got our just rewards for sneaking out. After that night, I forgot all about dreaming of the juicy loquats across the road. I still thought that it was wasteful to let them rot.

Soon it was nearing the end of third term and everyone was counting the number of sleeps we had left, omitting the Saturdays and Sundays to make the countdown seem less than it really was but it was good for our spirit. We were allowed to go into the city to buy Christmas presents to bring back home so I used my savings to do just that.

The day the boarders left to go home was filled with both happiness and sadness, some of them leaving for good, never returning, the others making plans to return a few days earlier in the next year, to spend a couple of days together before school began and to see whether there were any new boarders in our class. I knew that I'd be returning so Anne and I chose which part of the Junior's dorm we'd be in, near the Sisters' rooms or near the Leaving's dorm. Anne would be back at school before me and would get things ready. Being upstairs with the older girls would be a lot different than being downstairs with the younger, silly girls. This also meant that we'd be able to short-sheet a few beds for a change, payback time.

The night before I was to leave for Broome was a little exciting for me. I would be seeing my family and friends again, after nearly a year away. I was the only boarder left now and had the run of the place but didn't know what to do with all this spare time. So I packed and unpacked my suitcases about twenty times in the next few days before leaving. I think the nuns were anxious to see the last of the boarders so that they could get on with whatever nuns had to do. In the meantime, they had made arrangements for the local priest to take me to the airport and I had to be ready by 5am for the long winding drive down the hill, otherwise I'd miss the plane. I didn't want that to happen, so I stayed up all night. I wanted to be back home in Broome.

HOME
AT LAST

WHEN I STEPPED OFF THE AIRPLANE at Broome Airport, all I could see were the brown and black faces of my family and friends. I was oblivious to the sounds and faces of the other dozens of people anxiously waiting to see their children coming home from boarding schools, then tears of joy all around. It was good to be home. I heard the voices calling out Grange! Grange! My heart just sang sweetly in my ears. I knew that I wasn't forgotten.

My mum was standing there with a baby in her arms and my two brothers close by her side. The baby was my new sister, Margaret Helena. She looked like my brothers with their pitch-black wavy hair and bright eyes. She clung to Mum, fear of me showing in her face. Can't be that ugly, can I?

My friends came up to me, talking a mile a minute, saying things like:

'Gee, Grange, you look different and talk any kind goes, just like gardias.'

'You're game coming home with a crewcut.'

'You going pictures tonight?'

'You go swimming tomorrow? Me and you can go walking to big jetty.'

I was home all right, just hearing them talking Broome way again! I couldn't wait to tell them about the latest movies and the hit parade songs and the rock'n'roll craze hitting Perth.

One of the crazes that hit me was my hairdo, well, crewcut that girls were wearing in Perth. I had taken the bus trip into the city to a hairdresser's. My beautiful black curly hair was cut in a boy's style with about an inch of hair, cut like the flat top of a battle ship, with little left with the short back and sides. When I got back to the college, I stuck my beret over my head so that the nuns couldn't see what I'd done. I must have shocked a lot of my friends when I got off the plane in Broome but it grew back to normal in no time, thank goodness. Wearing that 'do' in Perth was completely different to having it in Broome.

My family were pleased with their small gifts but were more anxious for me to tell them about my year in Perth, and I wasn't going to let them down. They stayed for a couple of hours then I got ready to go to the pictures with my cousins. Of course we had to walk to the pictures, some things just don't change overnight!

I had almost eight weeks of holidays up my sleeves, but time seemed to slip away so quickly. The first few weeks were spent catching up with my friends and family, window shopping in town, visiting other friends at their homes or going to the big jetty to swim. Sometimes we hung around Wing's Store because there was a jukebox there and we could sit inside and order refreshments and listen to songs. At Streeter's, I haunted the newspaper and ice-cream stands because that was where Sally and Pearly worked and we just yapped and yapped when there was nobody around. There were benches where we could sit and between ice-creams and milkshakes, I usually ended up talking to the two sisters. When there was nobody around for me to walk to town, I rode Dad's bike to pick up the mail and small groceries and pack them in the stringed-net bags. No plastic shopping bags those days!

I was getting used to another baby in the house now. I had known that there was a new baby in the family but at school I hardly gave a thought to it. My family was hundreds of miles away. It wasn't as if I was actually there to see her born, as I was with Alex and Henry. She was like a real live doll and Barb and I carried her everywhere around the house. The only thing wrong about her was that she had a dummy in her mouth almost twenty-four hours a day like a permanent fixture. Only when she was being fed did I see her little mouth free of the dummy. If her dummy was lost, we had to run to Ellies Store to buy another one or two, to pacify her otherwise she'd scream all night and day. Reminds me now of the Simpson kid, Maggie, who sucks the eternal dummy. There was also a new pram in the house I noticed. Thank goodness Mum had done away with the cane pram because the new style prams were convertibles, from prams to strollers, easier to handle and collapsible when not in use.

During the Christmas break of 1957, weekly dances were held on Friday nights at the Embassy, a nickname given to the little school that housed the lower primary kids. Every boy and girl who was old enough and allowed to go went there. Even the kids who weren't allowed to go sneaked out to have a good time. Most of the kids had parent approval because the night was well organised and supervised by Father McKelson, young working people, volunteer parents and friends of the school community.

Those were the days when boys partnered girls in dancing and we all got a big thrill when the boys asked us to dance, especially the boys we fancied. We eagerly awaited the tap on the shoulders.

I really looked forward to those Friday night dances because they were so popular and well organised. There was no live band or jukebox, only an old HMV gramophone but it did a great job even though the vibrations made the needle jump many times, especially when we jived to the rock'n'roll beat. But who cared? Bill Haley and his Comets got no spell with 'Rock Around the Clock' and neither did Elvis with 'Jailhouse Rock'. There were many various artists but those two were the most popular with us. Some of the guys were really classy ballroom dancers, despite being only country amateur dancers. It was all thanks to the Sisters for teaching us.

I went shopping one day and spotted a pair of olive green flatties. I fell in love with them instantly. I didn't have much money on me to buy them but I tried them on anyway. The shoes fitted me just right and I imagined them on my feet when I went dancing. So I put them on layby and begged Mum to get them out for me when she had money. When she did take the shoes out I wore them to the Embassy and every dance night since. They were my dancing shoes. Well, I wore them until the soles were no longer soles. I cut cardboard paper and slipped them into the shoes so that I couldn't feel the thin soles. I sure made good use of the flatties but in the following year I graduated to high heels and learned how to walk and dance in heels.

I was a bit surprised at how my friends could jive because there were no televisions to show them how and they were pretty good at it. Because Danny Howard and I came from the city where everybody danced the latest steps, we ended up showing them the different steps by dancing together a couple of times. It was just great dancing at the Embassy.

There weren't many things going for the young people around town, not like the young people of the USA, actually. They seemed to have everything: drive-in movies, skating rinks, baseball, their own cars, pyjama parties and everything we saw in the movies. One can only imagine how things were back then compared to the American kids. We may not have had everything but the weekly entertainment kept the kids off the streets and out of mischief, even if it did mean that some of the people laughed and made fun of us trying to dance the American way.

Well, those were the days of rock'n'roll. It was alive. It was the fifties. It was the age of Elvis Presley, Bill Haley and Little Richard. The list goes on. That was when rock'n'roll legends were born and went on to live in the minds of the young and old and the stories passed on to our children. Being away at boarding school must have drawn out the shyness in me, somehow. We were restricted in all things rock'n'roll but now at home everything seemed free. I was back with my friends and we were caught up in the new craze going around the world. That was life back home in the late fifties. I lived rock'n'roll; I breathed rock'n'roll; I sang and danced rock'n'roll. The radio ran hot. I listened to new hits, buying new records, by mail order, to play at home or at my friends. I must have driven my mum and Aunty Susie mad with the loud music but they didn't say anything. Yes, we were all caught up in the great American way and sadly enough, it hasn't changed much. Our kids are doing almost the exact things we did, only to a larger extent. We didn't know what drugs were then.

I also spent a lot of time down the beach with my friends, doing the usual things that teenagers do at the beach, swimming and gasbagging, running messages between boyfriends and girlfriends, goolmadjing for each other and finally walking or riding bikes back home in groups.

It was a really great holiday break for me but I knew that it wouldn't last too long for I'd be going back to school very soon. So don't let anyone tell you that life begins at forty. It's just not true. Your childhood and teenage days are the best ever, being young and carefree, for you're only young once and very old forever.

LEAVING
TIME

IT WAS NOW THE NEW YEAR OF 1958 and before I knew it, Tracey Cox and I were winging our way back to Perth. She was joining me at St Brigid's and I was really glad to have some company from home. We were met by Father Lumen and taken to Pallottine Centre. This time I knew what to expect in Perth and I kind of looked forward to the year ahead.

My second year at St Brigid's was almost a repeat of the first year, with a few exceptions, of course. We were now living upstairs in the Juniors' dorm. It was good to see Anne and Pauline again and that afternoon we unpacked all our cases, made up our beds and settled in for the year. We decided not to short-sheet the other girls' beds that night but to do it the next night, catching them unprepared. Gosh, it felt great to get in first because they usually got us every time, before.

Tracey got along fine with the girls in her class and soon settled down to routine. I only wished that I could have had someone else with me in my first year away because it got lonely with nobody else from your country. There may be friends around but nothing compares to family and country.

I found that I now had to study more seriously because the subjects became harder and I did want to pass the Junior exams. I just had to, for myself and for the people who most supported Aboriginal education. I couldn't waste two years for nothing. So buckle down I did even though I still had my free times and good times with my friends.

My birthday was approaching fast and I realised that I wouldn't have my family and childhood friends to help me celebrate it. I was going to be sweet sixteen! All my friends at school knew when my birthday was. Mine was the first one for the year in our class and I was really looking forward to it.

In the days approaching, they began to ignore me in small

ways, not only Anne but the whole class. When they saw me coming their way, they side swept me and kept on going. It wasn't only one girl who avoided me but also when they were in two's and three's. I really felt it. I must have been the loneliest girl in the school apart from the lonely little first graders. I didn't feel right in telling Tracey. I didn't want to burden her with anything. She had her own friends and I couldn't spoil it for her. I had to handle it myself, this pain of mine.

On the morning of my birthday someone remembered and let the whole dorm know so at least my sixteenth birthday was acknowledged by my friends nodding their heads. Not even a do-it-yourself card for me from them, I asked myself? Didn't look like it so maybe later on I'd get a card.

When school was let out they left me for dead and headed back to the dorm. I went straight to the pool and sat around talking to the other girls but still keeping an eye out for them. They did not come down to the pool and it was dinner time before I saw them again. We stood in our lines and Sister Rose told us to 'shoosh' then she marched us in. Still no one said anything, just carrying on talking amongst themselves, ignoring me and I felt like crying. After grace we sat down and a couple of the girls excused themselves to go into the kitchen to help. It was their chore that night but I took little notice of it, I was too sad. So in came the trolley with the meals, starting at the top where the seniors sat until it stopped at our table. All of a sudden a loud cheer went up from our table and the girls brought in a birthday cake and all the goodies to eat, one each balloons and party hats and one each bottle of Fanta or Coke. I went all teary inside and relief swept over me. I had forgotten their snubbing of me and in that instance I knew why they did it without their telling me. They were my friends after all.

'We wanted to surprise you with a birthday treat and didn't know how to do it. Someone was bound to tell you and that would have spoilt the surprise. We know how close Anne and Teresa are to you and we made them swear not to tell, so we had to ignore you and plan it. We had to get permission from Sister Mary Rose to go to the shop and we didn't want you to tag along. It was hard for us, too and we're sorry we had to do it,' they all said in almost the same time. We were best of friends again.

In the May holidays I went down to the small town of Manjimup with Anne. Her dad picked us up in Money Street, West Perth, where he owned a house and a married couple looked after the place. We drove there in his truck and it was a wonderful trip. We played games to keep ourselves occupied, like who spotted the most red cars on the road or 'I Spy.' Never once did Mr Rijavec tell us to keep quiet for I'm sure we must have driven him mad, what with our laughing loudly in the cab, about any little thing.

Anne's family ran a small timber mill or something to do with the industry. Her sister Joy still lived with their parents and was engaged to an Italian guy, Franco Lovi, who loved to tease Anne. I loved listening to their bantering, sometimes in outbreaks of English, between the Italian and Yugoslav language, even though I didn't understand them. I could read their body language and facial expressions so well and knew it was only teasing. I could tell that the two sisters were very close to each other just by the way they spoke to each other and shared things with each other. Mrs Rijavec couldn't speak much English for me to understand but that was all right with me, after all I came from a multilanguage background myself.

TRACEY COX, ANNE RIJAVEC AND ME, ST BRIGID'S COLLEGE, 1957

The Rijavecs made me feel most welcome and took me along with them when visiting friends and relations. It must have seemed very unusual to people around Manjimup that an ethnic European family was hosting an Australian Aboriginal girl for the holidays. It didn't matter to any of us who we were or that we looked differently and spoke differently. Anyway, we did have some things in common, like eating and enjoying lots of spaghetti and pasta meals. I didn't know that there were so many ways to cook up delicious pasta dishes.

Manjimup and Pemberton were beautiful timber country and I enjoyed my stay there. Anne took me to Fonty's Pool and to town for shopping and to see the movies. On one occasion we went to their friend's small tobacco plantation to see how they operated their business. It was fascinating to learn how the tobacco was grown and treated, graded and packed. There were a few women and men working there, young and old.

Soon it was time for us to head back to Perth and Mr Rijavec drove us again, this time at night, so Anne and I slept all the way to Perth. We stayed in the Money Street house with the housekeeper for a few days until we went back to college. We went to several movies in the city and caught up with some school friends who were also waiting to get back to the college.

During the year I played netball again and was quite good at it despite my height, so I played centre for the rest of the season. I liked playing because we got out of the campus for a day and met a lot of new girls from other schools. Of course I was advised to give up the game when it got closer to the Junior Exams. Mother Celestine said that I had to study even harder because the people back home had high hopes for me and that it would be a great achievement for the Aboriginal cause. So I gave up the opportunity to play in the finals. Needless to say, I did feel a bit sorry for myself but life goes on and my sacrifice did pay off. I did quite well when the results were published in the new year.

August holidays found me at Henrieke's home in Queen's Park or QP as we called it. Her mum and dad were also very nice people. She had two brothers but only the younger brother Gerd stayed at home. He was only about ten, I think. Paul was working and had his own place. I only met him once and never encountered him again.

Somehow, it was different at Henrieke's. Don't get me wrong about my other host families. They were all wonderful. Maybe the suburbs lacked the wide open spaces of the country, or something. It was suburbia, I suppose. Everybody had their own little fenced-off blocks and not a big back yard to play in and have big mobs of kids over, only a small group of friends. Yeah, I liked the family atmosphere and somehow I always seemed to relate to the ethnic families of my friends.

I met a lot of Henrieke's friends around QP and Cannington so if we weren't hanging around her place, we'd be over at theirs, playing the latest records and dancing in the back yard. The rock'n'roll craze was still going strong and we all sang and danced to the beat. Sometimes we walked to the shops in the evening with her friends and just talked away outside or under the street lighting until they walked us back home. Other times we played records and danced at somebody's place, usually on the lawn at the back. Somehow it wasn't scary walking around QP in the 1950s.

We walked or caught buses to get around to places. We played jukeboxes in the shops or played coin-operated games there. Sometimes we went into the city to see a movie. Once we were going to have dinner in a city restaurant but lost each other in the crowd, so I caught a bus home and I didn't really know where to get off. I had to walk for about twenty minutes before I found my way back. I waited outside for Henrieke to arrive so that we could enter at the same time; no good upsetting her mum and dad about our misadventure. It was so cold outside and I told her so. The poor thing was worried about me too and wondered whether I got home safely. Back in our room we laughed our heads off and got our stories straight about the mix-up.

Most of the big church events were the same as the year before but I began to see if differently. We went to Aquinas College for the Feast of Christ the King celebration and really took notice of how many followers of Christ came to participate. There were hundreds and hundreds of people of different races coming to celebrate the one Christ the King. It was an amazing scene. How come I didn't take note of this last year? The different school children displayed their schools in full uniform, splendour and pride. They were easily identified by their colours and logos. Even the young seminarians were out in full force. We heard some of the Leaving girls mutter under their breath, 'What a waste,' wondering what they meant at that time.

It was a very long ceremony and so moving but we eventually got back home and crashed into our beds, still feeling the soreness in our legs.

Just as we did in St Mary's, St Brigid's also had annual concerts. The one the year before was all right, I guess as there was no bad feedback on it. It was another embarrassing scene for me at this concert. It was a dancing act and there were quite a few girls in the front and we had to keep changing places from the front to the back of the stage to give the other girls a chance to be seen by their parents. During the dancing, I could feel my suspender belt slipping down to my knees as the elastic must have snapped. Every time I got to the back line I tried to pull it up but in vain, it slipped right down to my ankles and my stockings got tangled up between my feet. Talk about 'how embarrassing' again, especially when the audience roared with laughter. All I could do was curtsy, step out of my shoes, pull the stockings off, throw shoes and stockings in the corner and dance barefoot for the rest of the dance act. We got a standing ovation. Maybe they thought it was part of the act but I certainly didn't.

Soon it would be exam time and we all started to knuckle down to study hard. Sometimes we all studied together, other times we went out separate ways into the library or our favourite corner of the playing field. Sometimes we almost bit each other's heads off for the smallest reasons then made up with us bawling our eyes out. All the senior girls sympathised with us and assured us that it was a 'Junior' exam thing that we had to go through. We would look back on this and laugh about it later on, the big voices of experience assured us. When we sat for our final exam and finished it, we knew that they were right. All of us Juniors made a pact on that last day. We would all meet up again in ten years time at St Brigid's for a reunion but it never happened. It's such a pity.

I didn't want to face my dearest friends for the last time. I knew I was chicken-hearted and was already crying but I really didn't want to say goodbye. I heard footsteps coming down the stairs and I thought it was the sisters, so I rushed out of the room only to find myself face to face with my two friends, Pauline and Anne. Well, that was it. Three of us made the loudest cries ever heard in the boarding school, I'm sure.

'You didn't think we'd leave without saying goodbye, did you?' they asked. 'You silly goose!'

We just hugged each other, bawled loudly and spluttered in gibberish language, making foolish promises (at that time they were genuine). We must have cried for about an hour until it was time for them to go. I couldn't bear to see them go away in their parents' cars. I spent the night alone, spilling tears for my friends and for myself, for I knew I wouldn't be back again but I had kept it to myself. I left St Brigid's College for good the very next day, catching the early morning plane back home.

Even though I felt sad on the plane I wanted very much to see the Broome crowd again. I missed them so much and the year was a long time for us all. There was a lot of catching up to do.

As usual my family and friends came to meet me and take

me home. I handed out the presents and put the Christmas gifts in the cupboard and warned the kids not to open the boxes. Christmas wasn't too long away, only about three weeks to go, so they had to be patient.

I had to see Father McKelson the next day and he confirmed that the Bishop had gone back to Germany to retire and I wouldn't be going back to college unless they could find other funds, for the Bishop had used his own money to sponsor my education and now he was gone. I don't think that any of us knew about that, the sponsoring, I mean. Despite the disappointment for me, all this opened up the way for the Pallottine Centre to expand and take on more Aboriginal students around the State to further their education and training in Perth.

Years down the track I often wished that Abstudy funding was available for us in the fifties. I was sure that if I had stayed on at school I could have passed the Leaving Certificate exams in 1960 and matriculated to enter university.

I set about looking for work but to no avail, so I spent the time at home, at the beach or at friends. The weekly dances at the Embassy went on and I still enjoyed them. It was great to see everybody there, the girls wearing their flared or hoop skirts with multiple layers of frilly petticoats or in matadors or pedal pushers. Life was great and I wished that we could stay young forever but everybody knows that life goes on and time ages people.

We still walked to the picture shows, went swimming and did all the things we had done before. I was even game to ride on a motorbike with friends. I used to be afraid of motorbikes.

It was a great, silly summer season in Broome, and I managed to get a casual job for a few weeks with the Broome Road Board as a typist.

By the time the end of January came along, there was still no full-time job for me though and I decided to go to Port Hedland and try there. My Aunty Betty wrote to Mum and said that there was a position for a telephonist with the Post Master General's Department and the exam was to be held in two weeks time, so I booked my fare.

On the plane I looked down at old Broome town feeling a bit sad for I was leaving home again, perhaps forever.

Goodbye the forties and fifties. Goodbye my wonderful, silly childhood.

GLOSSARY

barney	goanna
bindjin	coolamon (used for carrying babies)
binghi	(bing-hi) Asian name for black fellow
bublee	brother
bugul-bugul	mud skipper
bumbye	bye and bye
bugunjun	pregnant
bundagurr	blind boil
bundusang	partner with banker in playing kaja kaja
chiffa	Chinese lottery
Dhari	an old Ceylonese/Indian man's name
djirri	pourri pourri, black magic
gardia	white person (unisex)
goolmudjing	skiting, flirting
goombali	person with same first name
goomboon	marsh or mangrove monster
goomboo	wee wee, urine
goonbi	snotty
goondoo	shoulder-ride
goongra	native bush fruit
goonoor	species of native gum tree
gubinge	native bush fruit
gujud	ash from gum tree used in chewing tobacco mix
gum	as in gum from trees
gurajun	drunk, drunken state
gurry	beer or alcohol
jibalgru	native small bird
jidja	sister
jingerose	exclamation or expression of speech
jowidge	panties

jubul	diving
jujud	devil
kinduk	a sign (vision), interpretation of dreams for chiffa (Chinese lottery)
kubba kubba	Aboriginal dances for ceremonies or initiations
leret	cicada
linju	policeman
lulu	grandfather
magabala	native bush fruit
mayi	bush tucker
mimi	grandmother
moolidjin	chewing tobacco
mullamulla-eyed	pus-eyed
moonga	bush honey
munjung	mad, silly
Mymuna	girl's name
ngeera	devil
njili njil	native bush fruit
nyanyas	breasts
pasang	bet, placed in chiffa
pourri pourri	black magic, spells
wanagnurri	money
wurumbas	fast-flowing creek from rains like small flash floods
yarm	silly

PHOTOGRAPHIC ACKNOWLEDGEMENTS

Many of the photographs that appear in *Last Truck Out* are from private
collections. Thanks to Margy Dia, Honor Bin Salleh,
Leslie Crispin, Sally Demin, Owen Torres and Marilee Liddell for granting
permission to reproduce photographs;
also to Kylie Jennings (Broome Historical Society Museum),
Zofia Carter (Battye Library of WA), and Pauline Guerinoni
(St Brigid's College, Lesmurdie) for their help in sourcing photographs. Kind
permission to reproduce photographs has been received from the Broome
Historical Society Museum, Battye Library of WA
and St Brigid's College.
Photographs from these collections are as follows:

BATTYE LIBRARY OF WA
p6 5376B/32; p30 816B/B5675; p47 816B/B5678;
p66 816B/B5677; p60 006952D; p69 006951D;
p133 011414D; p160 010835D; p231 000231D.

BROOME HISTORICAL SOCIETY MUSEUM
p105 BM2007-322; p162 BM2006/1353.

ST BRIGID'S COLLEGE, LESMURDIE
p258.

CONTEMPORARY PHOTOGRAPHS

Photographs by Nigel Gaunt, Red Dirt Photography, Broome.

In order of appearance – Pandanus, Cape Leveque;
Storm on Cable Beach, Broome; Beagle Bay Church, Beagle Bay;
Bananas, Broome; Boab, East Kimberley; Trappist bell, Broome (originally
from Beagle Bay Mission); Rosary beads, Broome; Holding hands, Broome;
Aerial view of Broome 1; Shutters, Broome; Marsh house, Broome;
Backyards in Chinatown, Broome; Chinatown street sign, Broome;
Pearls and plumes, Broome; Angus fishing off Streeter's jetty at king tide, Broome;
Sun Pictures, Chinatown; Old Broome street signs, Broome;
Big sister and Junior, Broome; Marbles in the pindan, Broome;
Schoolyard in Broome; Beagle Bay Church, Beagle Bay; Two suitcases, Broome;
Flying over Streeter's jetty at king tide, Broome; Aerial view of Broome 2.